YOF

D0130190

The Prelude
and
Selected Poems

William Wordsworth

Notes by Martin Gray

 Longman

 York Press

The right of Martin Gray to be identified as Author of this work has been asserted by
him in accordance with the Copyright, Designs and Patents Act 1988

YORK PRESS
322 Old Brompton Road, London SW5 9JH

PEARSON EDUCATION LIMITED
Edinburgh Gate, Harlow,
Essex CM20 2JE, United Kingdom
Associated companies, branches and representatives throughout the world

First published 2003

ISBN 0-582-77228-1

Designed by Vicki Pacey
Phototypeset by Land & Unwin (Data Sciences), Northampton
Produced by Pearson Education North Asia Limited, Hong Kong

CONTENTS

PART ONE

INTRODUCTION   How to Study a Poem   5
               Reading Wordsworth's Poetry   6

PART TWO

COMMENTARIES   Note on the Text   10
               Simon Lee, the old Huntsman   10
               Anecdote for Fathers   13
               We are seven   14
               The Thorn   16
               The Idiot Boy   19
               Expostulation and Reply   22
               The Tables Turned   22
               Lines written a few miles above Tintern
                  Abbey   24
               'There was a boy'   31
               'Strange fits of passion'   32
               Song ('She dwelt among th' untrodden ways')   34
               A slumber did my spirit seal   35
               Michael: A Pastoral Poem   36
               Resolution and Independence   38
               Composed upon Westminster Bridge   42
               The Solitary Reaper   43
               My heart leaps up   47
               'I wandered lonely as a cloud'   48
               Ode   49
               'Surprised by joy, impatient as the wind'   53
               The Prelude: Books I–II   55
               Note on the Text   55
               Note on the Summaries   56
               Book First: Introduction   57
               Book Second: School-time   65
               The Prelude: Books III–XIII:
                  Short summaries   70
               Book Third: Residence in Cambridge   70
               Book Fourth: Summer vacation   73

Book Fifth: Books   75
Book Sixth: Cambridge and The Alps   79
Book Seventh: Residence in London
    and French Revolution   84
Book Eighth: Retrospect   86
Book Ninth: Residence in France   88
Book Tenth: Residence in London   90
Book Eleventh: Imagination   92
Book Twelfth: The same subject   98
Book Thirteenth: Conclusion   99

PART THREE

CRITICAL APPROACHES
            Lyrical Ballads and the 'Preface'   103
            Poetic Diction   106
            Nature and Pantheism   108
            Wordsworth and his Characters   112

PART FOUR

BACKGROUND   Wordsworth's Life   115
             Literary Background   118

PART FIVE

CRITICAL HISTORY
            Wordsworth and the Critics   120
            Textual Study   123
            New Criticism and After   123
              Biographical, Psychological and Historical
                Criticism   124
              Contemporary Criticism   125

PART SIX

BROADER PERSPECTIVES
            Further reading   127
            Chronology   129

Literary Terms   133
Author of these Notes   136

PART ONE

INTRODUCTION

HOW TO STUDY A POEM

Studying on your own requires self-discipline and a carefully thought-out work plan in order to be effective.

- Poetry is the most challenging kind of literary writing. In your first reading you may well not understand what the poem is about. Don't jump too swiftly to any conclusions about the poem's meaning.
- Read the poem many times, and including out loud. After the second or third reading, write down any features you find interesting or unusual.
- What is the poem's tone of voice? What is the poem's mood?
- Does the poem have an argument? Is it descriptive?
- Is the poet writing in his or her own voice? Might he or she be using a persona or mask?
- Is there anything special about the kind of language the poet has chosen? Which words stand out? Why?
- What elements are repeated? Consider alliteration, assonance, rhyme, rhythm, metaphor and ideas.
- What might the poem's images suggest or symbolise?
- What might be significant about the way the poem is arranged in lines? Is there a regular pattern of lines? Does the grammar coincide with the ending of the lines or does it 'run over'? What is the effect of this?
- Do not consider the poem in isolation. Can you compare and contrast the poem with any other work by the same poet or with any other poem that deals with the same theme?
- What do you think the poem is about?
- Every argument you make about the poem must be backed up with details and quotations that explore its language and organisation.
- Always express your ideas in your own words.

These York Notes offer an introduction to the poetry of William Wordsworth and cannot substitute for close reading of the text and the study of secondary sources.

During his lifetime – after about 1820 (when he was fifty years old) – Wordsworth was recognised as one of the great poetic voices of English literature. He was keenly read in Victorian households. To illustrate this, we need look no further than *Palgrave's Golden Treasury*, an immensely popular and influential anthology of verse that was first published in 1861, and reprinted many times: this collection contained no less than forty-four of his poems, more than any other poet except for Shakespeare.

In the latter quarter of the twentieth century Wordsworth's apparently unassailable reputation as a 'great poet' began to wane, although in suffering this fate he was by no means alone. During the 1970s the core tradition of English poets and novelists, which until then had served as the centre of every educational syllabus, was rejected by many university teachers as unsuitable for new generations of students; it was too elitist, too dominated by male writers, and too dedicated to writing from the past. Poets like Wordsworth were derided as 'dead white European males', shorthand for all that was deemed pernicious and unfashionable in the new order.

In Wordsworth's case this general unpopularity has probably been compounded by the trajectory of his political beliefs, from youthful revolutionary enthusiasm to conservative quietism. Wordsworth was a generation older than many of the other so-called **Romantic** poets, most of whom did not grow old: Keats died in 1821 of tuberculosis aged twenty-six, Shelley was drowned at sea in 1822 aged thirty, and Byron died of malaria in 1824 aged thirty-six, on his way to support the Greek war of independence against the Turks. Wordsworth was to live on until 1850, enjoying a dignified, lauded and 'lionised' old age, honoured by the establishment even to the point of being appointed poet laureate in 1843.

Now that he is no longer part of the core syllabus of literary study, Wordsworth is possibly less read than at any other time in the two hundred years since he started publishing his poems. Such is the limited appeal of poetry with the reading public, those who do read his work are, however, still most likely to do so as part of a programme of study, rather than for any intrinsic pleasure and value that might be found in his poems. Whoever his readers are, they are almost certain to arrive at his poems prejudiced by one simple but weighty opinion as to Wordsworth's poetic output: he is the poet who writes about Nature with a capital N – the mountains, lakes and trees of England's Lake District. Whether this prejudice works for or against Wordsworth may depend on the reader's own attitude to this kind of natural scenery. For the very many of us who live in towns and suburbs, Nature may represent either an idealised place of refuge, or a huge irrelevance.

It would be pleasant to be able to rebut this prejudice, but to do so would be another distortion. Wordsworth does indeed write about Nature, though in a way very peculiar to himself, and, when considered carefully, his descriptions of scenery shed light on the whole processes of perception and poetic creativity. He is not in any simple way a Nature poet, as the discussions of individual poems in this book will show.

If he finished his life as a conservative and establishment figure, this was emphatically not true of his early poetic career, which was in many respects innovative and ground-breaking (though perhaps less so than he claimed in his own critical writings). Wordsworth's career began in controversy – *Lyrical Ballads* was savagely attacked by the critics – and now he is once again part of a controversy, though one that is academic rather than current. If we are to understand contemporary and modern poetry, then we must look at nineteenth-century poetry, and this means we have to read Wordsworth. If we are to understand the history of twentieth-century criticism and the current and ongoing debates about what kinds of literature should feature in the examination syllabuses and university curriculum, then we must also read Wordsworth for ourselves, to determine where we stand in relation to these arguments, unless we are happy simply to accept wholesale the opinions of others.

These are serious reasons for reading Wordsworth's poetry, but they will only appeal to those already engaged with the study of poetry and criticism. There is a simpler reason: Wordsworth was an expert poet. He was a highly self-conscious writer, as his critical essays and comments show. Anyone who wants to see how the resources of language can be deployed to effect should read poetry, which uses the full resources of language in their strongest concentration, and Wordsworth's best poems can provide a master class in these techniques. Though he pretends sometimes to a rural simplicity, this is the result of the most careful and painstaking art. Even in his most cerebral and difficult writing, he wants to be understood by the general reading public who made up his audience during his lifetime. The idea of an obscure and esoteric poetry, cherished by only a few enlightened souls, would have displeased him immensely. He had a lofty sense of the absolute value and purpose of his writing. The 'Preface' to the 1800 edition of *Lyrical Ballads* is one of the great statements of the value and importance of poetry.

In the nineteenth century, readers of all kinds found consolation in Wordsworth. A famous expression of this restorative effect is that of J.S. Mill, the Utilitarian philosopher, in his *Autobiography* (begun in 1853 but published posthumously in 1873). He writes movingly of how significant Wordsworth was in helping him recover from a terrible depression:

> What made Wordsworth's poems a medicine for my state of mind, was that they expressed, not mere outward beauty, but states of feeling, and of thought coloured by feeling, under the excitement of beauty. They seemed to be the very culture of the feelings, which I was in quest of. In them I seemed to draw from a source of inward joy, of sympathetic and imaginative pleasure, which could be shared in by all human beings; which had no connection with struggle or imperfection, but would be made richer by every improvement in the physical or social condition of mankind. From them I seemed to learn what would be the perennial sources of happiness, when all the greater evils of life shall have been removed. And I felt myself at once better and happier as I came under their influence.

Wordsworth himself wrote his great autobiographical poem, *The Prelude*, in order to escape from a similar mood of desolation and despair. His poetry is infused with a sense of the ordinary sorrows of existence, the 'still, sad music of humanity' – the pain of loss and disappointment, growing old, the fear of death. He believed that such experience was universal to all humanity, an idea nowadays regarded as intrinsically dubious, as no more than the complacent assumption of the supremacy of the values of a particular and local culture. In his 'Preface' he describes his subject matter thus:

> But these passions and thoughts and feelings are the general passions and thoughts and feelings of men. And with what are they connected? Undoubtedly with our moral sentiments and animal sensations, and with the causes which excite these; with the operations of the elements and the appearances of the visible universe; with storm and sunshine, with the revolutions of the seasons, with cold and heat, with loss of friends and kindred, with injuries and resentments, gratitude and hope, with fear and sorrow.

This is the proper focus for poetry, according to Wordsworth. It may be that he makes such pleasurable poetic music out this spectrum of experience that he can console us too, make us feel, if only for a moment, 'better and happier', perhaps against all our preconceptions and cynicism. Wordsworth himself as a boy used to learn poems by heart and recite them out loud as he walked around Esthwaite Water. Such a primitive and naïve mode of enjoying poetry is now probably unusual, though learning by heart 'A slumber did my spirit seal' or 'The Solitary Reaper' would certainly be one way of understanding and absorbing those short lyrics. Learned like that, in a manner Wordsworth himself would have valued, who knows what their effect might be in a modern psyche? But even if his poetry never works any kind of magic on us, the effort of trying to understand how readers felt and reacted to the range of feeling and thought in Wordsworth's poetry should help us to exercise our historical imagination, and thereby enlarge the circumference of our knowledge and sympathy.

PART TWO

COMMENTARIES

NOTE ON THE TEXT

The text used is *William Wordsworth: Selected Poems*, edited by Damian Walford Davies, and published by Everyman, Dent and Tuttle, 1994. This edition includes useful Notes and extracts from critical writings about Wordsworth. Page numbers refer to this edition. The text used for *The Prelude* is taken from *Wordsworth: The Prelude – The 1805 Text* published by Oxford University Press, 1970.

SIMON LEE THE OLD HUNTSMAN
FROM *LYRICAL BALLADS*, 1798/1800 (pp. 76–8)

Helping an old man cut through a root

The poem describes Simon Lee, an old man who in his youth was a keen and joyful huntsman, famed for his speed as a runner. The master and inhabitants of the hall of Ivor, where he used to work, are all now dead, and the old huntsman is the only survivor from that past age. He now lives in extreme poverty with his aged wife, trying to keep himself alive by cultivating a small patch of land. He is half-blind and crippled by weak ankles, which are swelling painfully. His only present joy is listening to the sounds of the hunt, and he does not expect to live much longer. The poem finishes with a description of an incident in which the narrator finds Simon Lee trying to hack through the roots of a tree with a spade, and offers to assist him. The rotten wood, which the old man was labouring in vain to cut, is severed with a simple, single blow. At this help the old huntsman weeps in apparent gratitude, though the narrator seems puzzled at the strength of this reaction, and wonders what conclusions should be drawn from the incident.

This poem illustrates exactly that uneasy and unexpected mixture of **poetic genre** and **tone** hinted at in the title of the *Lyrical Ballads* (see p. 103), moving strangely from an apparently **narrative** beginning to the **first-person** address to the reader and account of the meeting between Simon Lee and the narrator. Throughout the first three **stanzas**, the jaunty rhythms and the choice of words – 'sweet' and 'pleasant', 'merry' rhymed with 'cherry', 'glee' chiming with 'Lee' – that are used at the start of the poem pull us towards an artificial ballad-like world, set far back in time. The hall of Ivor and the near-legendary capabilities of Simon Lee the huntsman in his youth appear sentimentally bathed in the glow of a far-off semi-legendary past. To begin with we are likely to gloss over the accumulation of oddities: Simon Lee is a little man (almost a gnome?), but 'I've heard he once was tall' (line 4). Later we realise how shrunken he is in physique and circumstance. Apparently meaningless redundant details fill out the lines to make easy rhymes – 'A long blue-livery coat has he,/ That's fair behind and fair before' (lines 9–10). The redundancy hints at the old man's pride in the garment that relates him to the past and his former attachment to wealth and a life of vivid activity, a sharp contrast with his present state: 'Yet, meet him where you will, you see/ At once that he is poor' (lines 11–12). All this comes to an end with a horrid finality in the third stanza, when we are told that no one now 'dwells' (the poem's second use of this poetic word) in the hall of Ivor: 'Men, dogs and horses, all are dead;/ He is the sole survivor' (lines 22–4).

His life as a huntsman has left Simon Lee with nothing materially. He has had to enclose his pathetic scrap of land from the common ground. Worse than nothing, he is half blind – which we understand is in some way related to his former prowess as a 'running huntsman merry' (line 14) – and crippled with weak ankles. Wordsworth dwells on the grotesque detail of the old man's swollen, thick ankles and thin legs, with a **realism** that is the very opposite of the apparently poetic, **sentimental** vision of the past in 'pleasant Ivor hall' (line 2). Such a mixture of tones is disturbing, almost shocking.

Yet Wordsworth plays with our expectations even more by a direct address to the 'gentle reader' (line 75) in the ninth and tenth stanzas. The narrator seems to be almost mocking in his refusal to present us with a 'tale' (line 76), and argues that if we seek such a narrative, then we have to make it ourselves. We are being warned that there must be more to this poem than its surface, in case we are simply puzzled or annoyed by its strange lurching between sentimentality and realism. Certainly he wishes to put us on our guard by reminding us of the self-consciousness and artificiality of the poem. Any thought that it was simply out of control must be reconsidered. He taunts us with his awareness that we are looking for some 'tale', some familiar patterns of narrative or morality that will put us at our ease, disturbed as we may be by those disgusting ankles, and the unavoidable focus on the poverty and decrepitude of Simon and Ruth Lee. If we think for ourselves, examining 'such stores as silent thought can bring' (line 74), we can find a tale everywhere, but the narrator is not going to provide it.

The poem moves on to its concluding incident, the narrator's meeting with Simon Lee, and the cheery ease with which he hacks through the root at which the old man 'so long/ And vainly had endeavoured' (lines 95–96). The old man weeps his 'thanks and praises' (line 98) and seems 'they never would have done' (line 100). The narrator concludes that not ingratitude but 'Alas! the gratitude of men/ Has oftener left me mourning' (lines 103–4). Where is the tale? What is the moral of the non-story, that we have been warned to look for? Clearly Simon Lee weeps for more than gratitude. The strength and, presumably, relative youth of the narrator, that allowed him to cut the roots with a single swipe, by contrast seems to have set the old man weeping for his weakness and uselessness. The narrator (and the poem) 'mourns' the contrast between active youth and poverty-stricken old age, the present and the past. But we are still left a little puzzled – does the narrator realise the implications of the help he has proffered the old man? It is as if he does not really understand why the old man is so upset. Is Wordsworth asking us to see beyond the narrator's cheerful and easy good turn, thoughtlessly delivered, into an understanding of loss and sorrow that is far greater than can be summed up by a single little moral reflection?

'Simon Lee' is written in eight-line stanzas, each of which is split into two **quatrains** consisting of three lines of **iambic tetrameter**, and a concluding line of iambic **trimeter**. Alternate lines are rhymed throughout the poem (*abab cdcd* etc.). This highly organised verse-form is handled with flexibility and freedom of expression, whether Wordsworth is using it to contain backward-looking ballad-like narrative, the direct address to the reader, or the narrative of the encounter with the old man.

Poems for comparison: 'Goody Blake and Harry Gill' (p. 70); 'Resolution and Independence' (p. 286)

9 **livery-coat** the uniform that identified Simon Lee as a servant and huntsman
38 **tillage** ploughing, cultivation
44 **stone-blind** completely blind (cf. 'stone deaf')
62 **enclosed** the fencing off of common or waste land that in feudal times had belonged to the community
85 **mattock** pick-like implement with blade set at right-angles, allowing it to be used for cutting

A NECDOTE FOR FATHERS: SHOWING HOW THE ART OF LYING MAY BE TAUGHT'   FROM *LYRICAL BALLADS*, 1798/1800 (pp. 79–80)

A conversation between a father and his young son

A father goes for a stroll with his five-year-old son. He is happy, and in his happiness he looks back to the place – Kilve – where he was also happy a 'long year' (line 12) ago in spring (though there may be a hint of unhappiness intervening). In idle conversation he asks his child whether he prefers Liswyn Farm, where they are now, or Kilve, where they were. His son replies that he prefers Kilve. The father seems annoyed at this reply and asks the little boy repeatedly why he has expressed this opinion. The child, unable to explain his preference, sees a wind-vane and picks on this as an explanation: 'At Kilve there was no weather-cock,/And that's the reason why' (lines 55–6). This illogical reply teaches the father a lesson.

Commentary about this poem is combined with 'We are Seven' which follows immediately

7 **intermitted** occasional
10 **Kilve** small town in Somerset

WE ARE SEVEN   FROM *LYRICAL BALLADS*, 1798/1800 (pp. 81–3)

A young girl thinks of her dead siblings in a deluded way

The poet-narrator describes meeting a young girl and asks her how many brothers and sisters she has. She answers that there are seven, including herself: two at sea, two in Conway, and two lying in the churchyard. The narrator questions her calculation, hinting that there are really only five of them. The girl presents the same explanation. The narrator insists they are only five. The girl explains how she spends her time in the churchyard, and how a sister and then a brother died, and are buried there. She is asked yet again to count, but maintains 'we are seven' (line 64). Exasperated, the narrator insists that two of them are dead, but the girl continues in her belief that she and her siblings number seven.

> These two poems, offering an oblique look at the relative wisdom of children and adults, are so close in technique and theme that it is convenient to discuss them together. Both share the same metrical form, a quatrain consisting of three lines of iambic tetrameter and a final concluding line of iambic trimeter, rhymed *abab*. This offer a simple, almost sing-song structure, though the final rather heavy line of each stanza is often used to underline the conflicting points of view that are the subjects of both poems, for example, 'Then ye are only five' (line 36) and 'O master! we are seven' (line 64) in the poem of that name. What characterises these anti-rational verses is Wordsworth's development of the poet-narrator, the first-person speaker of the verse, as a **persona** whom we should perceive ironically. In both poems we are supposed to realise that the adult's apparent rationality is exposed as hollow or cruel by a childish view of the world.

> In the final stanza of 'Anecdote for Fathers' the father understands his mistake. His interrogation of his son, initiated 'in very idleness' (line 20), over a subject of no apparent importance – which place does the boy prefer – has led the child to search for a specious explanation by which to explain a 'careless' (line 33) opinion. The choice of the weathercock is highly suitable as its purpose is to respond to the changing winds and weathers, just as the boy has to suffer his father's alteration of mood.

It might be that there is some particular reason why the boy prefers past Kilve to present Liswyn Farm that annoys his father – these places are separated by a 'long, long year' (line 12), and there is a strange stanza which hints oddly at some intervening pain:

> A day it was when I could bear
> To think, and think, and think again;
> With so much happiness to spare,
> I could not feel a pain. (lines 13–16)

Thought seems to imply pain, and happiness is felt in the context of painful feelings. Whether the boy's opinion is a truthful reflection of some painful period, or is simply an idle reply to an idle question does not matter. The adult's strangely forceful insistence on a logical explanation for this opinion seems to destroy the good mood of the morning, and forces the child into a desperate 'lie', so obviously meaningless that it brings the father up short and makes him realise his own folly.

In 'We are Seven' by contrast the adult-narrator never realises the cruelty of his own equally insistent questioning. The girl insists that she co-exists with her dead siblings, and by doing so implicitly keeps their memory alive in a way that brings her pleasure and helps her come to terms with her loss. The narrator's protests become progressively harsher till the final stanza: 'But they are dead; those two are dead!' (line 65). Why should he persist so in wanting to deprive a small girl of her visionary acceptance of death, when he had nothing to offer except an adult view of death as terminal loss and blankness?

Many of Wordsworth's poems deal in different ways with childhood. These two poems show that adults, caught in the mind-set of logic and rationality, might often learn from the apparent irrationality of 'childishness'.

Poem for comparison: 'Characteristics of a Child three years old' (p. 323)

15

THE THORN   FROM *LYRICAL BALLADS*, 1798/1800 (pp. 84–91)

The story of an eerie thorn bush and the woman who weeps there

A narrator describes an aged thorn bush, covered in lichen, which grows high in the mountains near a path and a small pond. Also nearby is a bright and colourful patch of moss, the size of a baby's grave. Travellers must be careful crossing the mountains near this thorn bush, for sometimes a woman sits there, crying 'Oh misery! oh misery!' (line 65). She is there, we are told, in all weathers. The narrator warns us that no one dares visit the spot near the thorn bush when she is there – you have to make sure she is in her hut if you wish to see it. Why does this woman visit the spot? The narrator undertakes to tell us all he knows, but recommends that we visit the thorn bush in order to understand the woman's story. The woman's name is Martha Ray, and she was once betrothed to Stephen Hill. But he marries another. She is rendered mad with grief, and, it is rumoured, she is pregnant. She takes to visiting the mountain top. No one knows what happened to the baby. People heard strange voices coming from the mountains. The narrator asserts that it is a fact that Martha Ray sits by the thorn because he has seen her there himself, during a wild storm when he was seeking shelter. He heard her crying 'oh misery!' as the breeze ripples the water of the pond. What do the storm, the pond, the hill of moss and the wind mean? The narrator does not know for certain, but everyone agrees that the baby is buried under the moss. He does not believe that the woman would have killed her infant. Some people say you can see the baby's face in the pond. Some want to dig up the baby and bring the woman to justice, but they are prevented by the moss stirring and the ground shaking. The thorn is being dragged to the ground by the heavy moss. He repeats that the woman sits there at night, crying 'O woe is me! oh misery!' (line 253).

> This is a very peculiar poem, and opinion may be divided about its success. It is exactly that kind of awkward mixture of genre that characterises the *Lyrical Ballads* (see section on the *Lyrical Ballads*, p.103). It is a narrative poem, but one which dwells on the feelings, doubts and anxieties of a narrator, and is very far in mood from the anonymous and unemotional atmosphere of the ballads, in which

dreadful events are related without comment. Also unlike the ballads it has rather a complicated stanza form and rhyme scheme: each stanza has eleven lines, in which all the lines consist of iambic tetrameter, except for the fourth and the ninth lines, which are iambic trimeter. Its rhyme scheme is *abcb deff egg*. It looks as if it might fall into two quatrains and a triplet. However, this does not happen, because the second quatrain is connected to the triplet by rhyme and the fact that both contain couplets; and the first quatrain is connected to the triplet by the shared lines of trimeter. This is a strangely elaborate pattern for a narrative poem.

But it is only a narrative poem of a peculiar kind, because nothing very much happens. By the sixth stanza (of seventeen) we are told the basic facts of the poem. The thorn, the pond, and the small grave-sized hill of moss, have all been described in detail; such detail that they start to acquire symbolic significance: the ancient, gnarled, knotted quality of the tree is in strong contrast with the dull puddle and the lurid colour of the moss. We have been told of the woman who sits moaning there in all weathers, and we have all the clues necessary to guess her story. But instead the narrator labours to fill in the details, such as he can, though no one knows for certain what happened. The woman's story is exactly as we might have surmised, though all is uncertain, eerie, and overlaid with the narrator's superstitious fears and wonder. Unlike a ballad, it has no forward direction, but mulls over the same images. Almost every element of the poem is repeated, often several times. The complicated, interlaced metrical form Wordsworth has chosen for the poem matches this obsessive repetition.

Indeed the repetitive quality seems to indicate that we should see the narrator not as the usual poet-speaker, but as some other kind of person. He seems obsessed with the eerie spot that has captured his imagination, even to the point of offering boring detail:

> I've measured it from side to side:
> 'Tis three feet long and two feet wide. (lines 32–3)

Lines of this kind are often cited to illustrate how dull and banal a poet Wordsworth can be. Yet there is an explanation for this humdrum observation.

In the midst of the 'narrative' there is, rather surprisingly, an **interlocutor**, who asks questions of the narrator (stanzas 8, 10 and 20). This, the poem's repetition, and other props in the poem, such as the telescope in stanza 17, suggest that Wordsworth is trying to enter the psychology of another person, and the poem is as much about the state of mind of the narrator, who is not Wordsworth, as it is about the mad Martha Ray, or even the mountain-top location of her misery. It is in fact a **dramatic monologue**, an early example of the most influential poetic genre in the nineteenth and twentieth centuries, used extensively by Tennyson, Browning, and Pound and Eliot, amongst many others.

In his 'Preface' to the second edition of *Lyrical Ballads* Wordsworth makes it clear that this poem was an experiment in a new genre, and that he had a superstitious and repetitive narrator of a particular kind in mind. This argument was derided by the critic Jeffrey in an attack on Wordsworth's poetry in the *Edinburgh Review* for April 1808:

> … he thinks it indispensably necessary to apprise the reader, that he had endeavoured to represent the language and sentiments of a particular character – of which character he adds, "the reader will have a general notion, if he has ever known a man, *a captain of a small trading vessel*, for example, who, being *past the middle age of life*, has retired upon *an annuity, or small independent income*, to some *village* or country town, of which he was *not a native*, or in which he had not been accustomed to live!"

> Now, we must be permitted to doubt, whether among all the readers of Mr Wordsworth (few or many), there is a single individual who has ever had the happiness of knowing a person of this very peculiar description; or who is capable of forming any sort of conjecture of the particular disposition and turn of thinking which such a combination of attributes should be apt to produce. To us, we will confess the *annonce* appears as ludicrous and absurd as it would be in the author of an ode or an epic to say, "Of this piece the reader will necessarily form a very erroneous judgment, unless he is apprised, that it was written by a pale man in a green coat – sitting cross-legged on an oaken stool – with a scratch on his nose, and a spelling dictionary on the table."

We may choose to agree with Jeffrey that 'The Thorn' is an experiment that is not wholly successful, but the anger of his attack suggests just how surprising and experimental *Lyrical Ballads* was. Before we reject Wordsworth as a writer of banalities, we still need to understand that he may be a more oblique and subtle poet than sometimes appears.

Poems for comparison: 'The Complaint of a forsaken Indian Woman' (pp. 110–12)

THE IDIOT BOY   FROM *LYRICAL BALLADS*, 1798/1800 (pp. 92–105)

A thrilling journey for Johnny Foy

The owls cry out on a clear March night. Why is Betty Foy bustling around, putting her beloved idiot boy on horseback? He is clearly not capable of riding the horse. Betty's neighbour, Susan Gale, who lives on her own, is ill. Betty's husband is away cutting wood. This is why she has fetched their pony, and set up her boy to ride it: he must fetch the doctor or else poor Susan Gale may die. She has told Johnny many times what he has to do; not least, he must come home. Johnny is too excited to reply. He is so overcome with happiness at riding the pony that he forgets to guide it in any way. Betty is also thrilled to see her son riding off, and she is pleased to hear him mumbling excitedly to himself as he rides out of sight. The owls make their noise and Johnny makes his.

The horse is a gentle and well-behaved creature, but it does not know what is going on. Betty comforts Susan. But gradually she starts to worry about Johnny. Betty keeps guessing how soon it will be before Johnny and the doctor returns. Midnight passes and still no Johnny. Betty starts to complain at her son's laziness. By one o'clock she is really worried that Johnny has come to harm. She explains her fears to Susan, who encourages her to search for Johnny. He is nowhere to be found. All sort of terrifying possibilities enter her mind as to what might have befallen him. She wakes up the doctor who is angry. In her terror and alarm she forgets to send the doctor to Susan Gale. She still cannot find Johnny anywhere on the road, and in her misery even contemplates suicide. It occurs to her that the pony may have gone where it usually goes, to the wood, so she rushes off there.

The poet suddenly addresses the reader directly: who knows what has been going on in Johnny's mind during this exciting night? What imaginative adventures has he had? Even the muses of poetry cannot tell.

There by a waterfall is Johnny, sitting on the horse while it feeds. Betty is overcome with joy, to be reunited with her idiot boy. Dawn is breaking as they make their way back home. On the road they meet Susan Gale. As she grew more alarmed at what might have happened to Johnny, so her illness departed, and she has set off to help look. She is overjoyed to meet them, both safe. The owls are still hooting as they return home. Betty wants to know what Johnny has heard and seen on this night of moonlight and owls. He makes his proud reply:

> The cocks did crow to-whoo, to-whoo,
> And the sun did shine so cold. (lines 460–1)

What seems to interest Wordsworth in this poem are the different states of mind of mother and son, the first articulated in language, but subject to overconfidence, doubt, anxiety, fear, while the idiot boy remains joyful and unperturbed by the events of the night, though his state of mind is ultimately unfathomable. What he does manage to articulate, his summing up of his experience with which the poem ends, serves by its strangeness to remind us how differently he understands the world, yet his mental and linguistic processes are something we recognise as a method of apprehension. His statement is a kind of poem, much shorter than Wordsworth's, and more memorable, that sees the owls metaphorically as cocks, and the moon as a cold sun. Perhaps Wordsworth wants to demonstrate that the poetic impulse, a core means of understanding and interpreting experience, may be more readily available to the mentally disadvantaged, than to the adult intelligence, thick as it is with habit.

The mental disability of the 'idiot' boy is not sentimentalised – in spite of his mother's doting pride, he completely fails his commission to fetch the doctor. We are moved by his mother's unconditional love. The poem is jauntily confrontational. From its title onwards it is unsparingly straightforward in its depiction of Johnnie's incapacities, though this is repeatedly seen in the context of Betty's love for him. Even her aberration, her idea that he might be able to fetch the doctor, grows out of the conflict between this unstinting love, and love of her neighbour. One could hardly look for a better model for human behaviour than is related in this strange, mawkish and almost meaningless episode, which dwells on the mistakes of people on the bottom rung of society.

Betty's love is unconditional but she is shown to have moments of doubt about her son, and in her anguish at her neighbour's illness casts 'vile reflections' (line 168) on his character when he fails to bring back the doctor. But this soon changes to terror at the thought that he might be lost, even dead. The excess of her joy at finding him again is spelled out at length, and is even comic in its intensity: rushing to kiss him, she almost overturns the horse. The poet slyly reminds us of her former short burst of irritation by asking whether Johnny laughs 'in cunning or in joy' (line 388) at his mother's discomfiture, but 'cunning' suggests capacities that have no place in the moral vocabulary of the poem. 'You've done your best, and that is all' (line 408) is Betty's forgiving conclusion to the episode.

Does the poem sentimentalise the redemptive power of love? It is somehow absurd that Susan Gale, whose illness triggers the events of the poem, is shown to be cured by worrying about Johnny's welfare, and heaves herself from her sickbed to look for them both. Or is this just part of the poem's curious comedy? If we are motivated to laugh at these folk, does that make the poet's attitude to be superior and condescending? Perhaps this is a question that the poem asks us to consider: is this the language and point of view appropriate to the rawness of its subject matter?

How shocking Wordsworth's material – paupers, children, madness, idiocy – must have seemed to the original reader of *Lyrical Ballads*. His language also must have struck an audience accustomed to the polite veil of **poetic diction** as surprisingly direct. 'The Idiot Boy' is part of an experimental programme to change the focus of poetry that characterises Wordsworth's early work. In the strange passages at the heart of the poem just before the discovery of Johnny, the poet-narrator directly speaks to the reader. In the interests of pursuing 'a delightful tale' (line 326), he supplies a number of fanciful possibilities as to what the boy might have imagined. But in the end he denies that it is possible to offer any insight into what has happened. Jokingly, he complains that the 'gentle Muses' (line 349) of poetry repel his 'suit' (line 353) to know exactly what 'strange adventures' (line 351) befell the idiot boy, and then the poem simply moves on. This playing with his audience's expectations shows how self-conscious was Wordsworth's challenge to the perceived proprieties of poetry of his day.

Poems for comparison: 'Peter Bell, A Tale in Verse' (pp. 328–62)

EXPOSTULATION AND REPLY   FROM *LYRICAL BALLADS*, 1798/1800 (pp. 106–7)

A dialogue about doing nothing

'Why are you dreaming and doing nothing, William? Why not read a book and profit from knowledge of dead authors? You seem to look on the world as if you had no past and no responsibilities, like Adam.' So asks Matthew.

William replies: 'Even when we're doing nothing, our senses are working. I believe that there are influences in the world that we can pick up by being passive. Things come to us anyway, so that we don't need always to be actively seeking them. This is why I sit here and do nothing.'

22 **impress** meaning both 'being impressive' and 'pressing in' (expressing therefore the active aspect of nature, though in an ambiguous way)

Commentary about this poem is combined with 'The Tables Turned' which follows immediately.

THE TABLES TURNED   FROM *LYRICAL BALLADS*, 1798/1800 (pp. 107–8)

Down with books!

Leave those books alone. It is a beautiful evening. There is more wisdom in birdsong than in books. Nature is a better teacher, from whose wealth you can learn cheerfulness. There is more to be learned from woods than from book-learning. Too much analytical thought destroys the wholeness of natural beauty. Close those books and open your heart to nature.

13 **throstle** thrush
30 **barren leaves** the dry and dead leaves of books, in other words 'pages'

These two poems can best be treated as a pair. The second offers a more complete reply to Matthew's complaint in the first, about the poet's apparent idleness. Here Wordsworth attempts a completely different kind of poem than the semi-narrative pieces dealt with so far. The poetry moves towards the **sententious**. He is aiming to express some of his ideas in a language that is weighty and memorable in phrases such as 'wise passiveness' (line 24), 'this mighty sum / Of things forever speaking' (lines 25–6, 'Expostulation and Reply'), and 'Our meddling intellect / Misshapes the beauteous forms of things. / We murder to dissect' (lines 26–8, 'The Tables Turned').

What are his arguments? Wordsworth puts forward the view in many of his poems that nature, the world of things, but especially the countryside, is not a blank, dead background to human activities, but is in an active inter-relationship with humans who inhabit it: 'there are powers, / Which of themselves our minds impress' (lines 21–2). The world, 'the mighty sum of things' is 'forever speaking' (lines 25–6, 'Expostulation and Reply), to those who are wise enough to listen. ('Things' is almost a favourite word for Wordsworth; it is often how he refers to the world around us.) Across his poetry he offers a whole spectrum of more or less confident views about this active aspect of nature. In these poems he seems very sure that 'powers' emanate from natural objects:

> One impulse from a vernal wood
> May teach you more of man,
> Of moral evil and of good,
> Than all the sages can. (lines 21–4, 'The Tables Turned')

Considered scientifically, as Wordsworth would probably accept, this is nonsense. Morally educative vibrations do not emanate from woods. But considered as an exaggerated, semi-metaphorical way of saying that human beings in a modern world need constantly to see themselves in relation to the natural world – vegetation, the weather, wild animals, and the cycle of the seasons – in order to achieve a balanced view of humanity and its role on earth, then what the poems seek to argue is readily acceptable. The idea that the human 'meddling intellect' (line 26) as employed in 'science and art' (line 29) often loses perspective on the wholeness of experience and knowledge is now almost a cliché: 'we murder to dissect' (line 28, 'The Tables Turned') has acquired an almost proverbial quality.

It is, of course, ironical that Wordsworth should use poetry – heightened language which though not exclusively book-bound, being written to be spoken out loud, is most usually found on the dry leaves of books – for an attack on books, reading and academic wisdom. Once again he overturns convention in *Lyrical Ballads*, attacking the sterile rigours of study, and proposing the true value of taking pleasure in scenery and songbirds, and allowing the mind to drift. Wordsworth seems always practical rather than mystical – these are not vague poems at all – but there is a strong respect for irrationality that motivates his narratives, but also his didactic writing.

Poems for comparison: 'Two April Mornings' (pp. 138–40); 'The Fountain' (pp. 140–2)

LINES WRITTEN A FEW MILES ABOVE TINTERN ABBEY: ON REVISITING THE BANKS OF THE WYE DURING A TOUR JULY 13, 1798 (Hereafter called in these Notes 'TINTERN ABBEY')
FROM *LYRICAL BALLADS*, 1798/1800 (pp. 114–18)

A meditation on memory and landscape

Once again, after five years, I am looking at this picturesque landscape, encompassing the river, wild cliffs, the sky, woods, farmland, and wood-smoke, a sign of human presence.

In the intervening years, memories of these sights, 'these forms of beauty' (line 24) have not been merely blank or abstract. In the city, I have remembered them with pleasure. Unconsciously also they may have affected my feelings, and perhaps in this way have influenced my behaviour so as to make me a better, more generous person. Another special gift comes from these memories, a 'blessed mood' (line 38) in which the world about us, which so often seems a weary, mysterious, unintelligible burden, instead is experienced with a profound sense of harmony, joy and understanding: 'we see into the life of things' (line 50).

Perhaps this is a false idea; but even so many times when depressed by the dreary round of ordinary life, I have often returned in spirit to you, River Wye.

Now, in a puzzling way, the memories are brought to life again by the scenery before me, and I am now aware that this will provide pleasing memories for the future too. This is what I hope, even though I have changed greatly since I first saw these hills. In those days I was like a deer, going where 'nature' (line 73) seemed to lead me, but more as if I was escaping something I feared than approaching something I loved. In boyhood nature to me was in itself wholly fulfilling. I loved the forms of nature passionately – waterfalls, rocks, mountains, woods – without needing to explain or justify this love. The 'dizzy raptures' (line 86) of childhood are now gone, though I am not moping about their loss. Other gifts have taken their place. I now look on nature less thoughtlessly, hearing rather the 'sad music of humanity' (line 92). And I have felt and thought of a disturbing but joyful 'presence' (line 95): this is an energy or spirit that is everywhere in the world, including in the human mind. So I am still a lover of meadows, woods and mountains, and everything that we see and hear, the world, which is both half perceived and half created by our senses. I recognise that Nature and the senses are my guide and the key to my 'moral being' (line 112).

Even without the help of nature, my inspiration would not diminish, for you are with me, dear friend, and I see in your excited eyes something of my former enthusiasm. I see what I used to be in you, dear sister. I will pray, knowing that Nature will not betray her followers, but lead us on to joy, for Nature can so shape the mind that all the nastiness of daily life cannot deprive us of our confidence that the world is a blessed place. Let the moon shine and the winds blow on you. Later in life, your present ecstasy will mature and your mind will be full of lovely memories, so that if you should be depressed you will remember me and my prayer with healing thoughts. Even if I should no longer be able to see and hear you, then you still will not forget that we stood together by this river, and that I, so long a worshipper of Nature, came here with ever yet more love and zeal. Nor will you forget that after years away, this landscape was still more pleasing to me, both for its own sake, and for your sake too.

This is a long and difficult poem, quite unlike other material from

Lyrical Ballads, written in a language that is both dense and metaphorical, and through which Wordsworth expresses philosophical and psychological ideas which in themselves may be difficult to grasp, not least because the poet is himself grappling to understand them. In its concerns – the perception of the natural world in childhood and adulthood, the value of memory, the precarious balance of misery and hope, the relationship of the past, the present and the future – and in style and form (**blank verse**) it anticipates *The Prelude*.

Everyone who knows anything about Wordsworth knows that he is a poet of nature. In this poem he declares that he is a 'worshipper of Nature' (line 153), with his love and zeal reaffirmed by his visit to the Wye Valley, and his sister's excitement at its beauties. Is he then simply a Pantheist, who sees nature as a sort of god or goddess, and worships God in and through nature? Certainly in this poem, in the fourth large verse paragraph, Nature is capitalised and **personified**. He recognises that Nature and the 'language of the sense' (line 109) is:

> The anchor of my purest thoughts, the nurse,
> The guide, the guardian of my heart, and soul
> Of all my moral being. (lines 110–12)

But this is the conclusion of a complex and difficult argument that the poet wrings out of a puzzled confrontation with his memory and his perception that his pleasure in the natural world has changed since the careless happiness of youth. The poem is riddled with an overbearing sense of misery. The wonderful repetition of its opening lines ('five' three times; 'length' and 'long'; 'years' split into 'summers' and 'winters') sets the tone of the poem:

> Five years have passed! five summers, with the length
> Of five long winters… (lines 1–2)

Against the extreme pleasure at seeing and describing the 'forms of beauty' (line 24) before him, the poem seems to take it for granted that ordinary day-to-day existence is likely to be characterised by misery. A few such instances are listed:

'the heavy and the weary weight / Of all this unintelligible world' (lines 40–1)
'the fretful stir / Unprofitable, and the fever of the world' (lines 53–4)
'the still, sad music of humanity' (line 92)
'evil tongues, / Rash judgements, ... the sneers of selfish men' (lines 129–30)
'The dreary intercourse of daily life' (line 132)
'solitude, or pain, or fear, or grief' (line 144)

Many of the poem's arguments are expressed through negatives: 'no', 'not', 'nor', 'un-'. The poem is built around wonderfully described moments of confidence in the beneficence of the natural world – 'the deep power of joy' (lines 42–50) and the 'sense sublime / Of something far more deeply interfused' (lines 94–108). These are not easy, cheerful assertions, but statements powerfully wrung from the poet in an attempt to put into language a confrontation with experience that includes the fraught, the miserable and the problematic. As with the uneven balance of 'five summers' against 'the length / Of five long winters', the reader may feel that the force of the negative aspects of the poem seems to belie its positive arguments.

As mentioned above, at the climax of the poem's positive argument, Nature is personified as if it was a separate active entity with godlike characteristics, the object of love and worship. This personification is of course a literary device, a metaphor, a construction of language; Wordsworth as a poet knows this well. He stretches language to express the feelings and ideas that justify this personification. In the surrounding discussion he never lets go of the degree to which this perception is based in the senses:

> ... all the mighty world
> Of eye and ear, both what they half create
> And half perceive. (lines 106–8)

The world is possessed by the 'eye and ear'; 'things' only exists in the activity of perception, in inter-relationship with humans who see and hear them. Here Wordsworth makes it clear that he knows that he himself is both perceiving and creating Nature as a beneficent entity. It is not simply out there, waiting to be worshipped (he does not envisage Nature as a classical god, Pan, for example). The poem is a willed meditation on this act of perception mixed with creation, and an example of its achievement.

For a poem that is about the poet's relationship with the natural world, there is actually not a great deal of description of nature. The first verse paragraph is taken up by a rapt account of the panorama he sees before him. 'Tintern Abbey' is an example of the **prospect poem**, a chiefly eighteenth-century genre in which a landscape is described and moral reflections are attached to it. Wordsworth takes the genre into new realms of speculation. The form leaves its descriptive aspect quite quickly to become a meditation on epistemology – how knowledge of the world is acquired – and psychology – how experience is stored in the form of memory and utilised in the mind. However, his discussion is never so abstract that it loses its sense of firm location in the poet's personal experience.

After the first section, nature is not described precisely, but generalised into a kind of shorthand for the 'forms of beauty' (line 24): 'the sounding cataract ... the tall rock, / The mountain, and the deep and gloomy wood' (lines 77–9). Indeed, since Wordsworth's reputation is as a poet of nature, in his work there is surprisingly little meticulous depiction of nature for its own sake. Perhaps it would be more accurate to call him a psychological poet, a poet of the mind, whose particular mind is furnished with natural objects. Wordsworth is always very precise about the relationship between the different elements of his consciousness, the varied furniture of his mind – present perceptions, mood, feelings, memories, ideas, moral preconceptions, hopes and fanciful imaginings. Reading through 'Tintern Abbey' demonstrates that the poem is careful to show the relationships between these different mental functions, while showing them functioning together. Again it is worth stressing the way that his abstract ideas are firmly located in the description of an experience which achieves a strong sense of authenticity. Whether or not he is exactly authentic is a matter for conjecture; and whether exactitude matters anyway is open to debate (see the discussion of 'The Solitary Reaper', pp. 43–7). In this respect he deserves to be remembered as an autobiographical poet, rather than primarily a poet of nature.

His excellence as a poet, however, must depend on his skilful use of language rather than on his interest in psychological speculation or his pantheistic leanings. 'Tintern Abbey' exhibits a large variety of different kinds of language, but it is full of passages where Wordsworth shows a remarkable and thrilling expertise. Here is one example, the climax of the poem's argument:

> ... I have felt
> A presence that disturbs me with the joy
> Of elevated thoughts: a sense sublime
> Of something far more deeply interfused,
> Whose dwelling is the light of setting suns,
> And the round ocean, and the living air,
> And the blue sky, and in the mind of man –
> A motion and a spirit that impels
> All thinking things, all objects of all thought,
> And rolls through all things. (lines 94–103)

This single sentence illustrates the poet's skill with **blank verse**, and in his choice of words and metaphorical expression.

The grammar of the sentence is wonderfully fluid and various in relation to the verse line: four of the lines are examples of enjambment; they are run-on with no grammatical pause at the end of the line; and six are end-stopped, with pauses signalled by the punctuation. Four of the lines have breaks in the middle, also signalled by the punctuation. So there is a pleasing variety of units of meaning, with the longest running over three lines ('I have felt …thoughts'); two over two lines but distributed differently ('a sense … interfused', a half plus one line); ('A motion … things', a line plus a half); the remaining units of sense are all half lines. Such pleasing variety and flexibility prevents the blank verse from falling into repetitive grammatical and rhythmical patterns.

More amazing is Wordsworth's extraordinary turn of phrase in this climactic passage. He has 'felt' a 'presence' that 'disturbs' him with the 'joy' of 'elevated thoughts'. 'Presence' is vague – what he is trying to describe is abstract, evanescent and tenuous rather – but the movement from feeling to thought, and the strange conjunction of joy, disturbance and 'elevated' thought is itself disturbing. The language continues to locate ideas in feelings by unusual combinations of the general and the abstract. He feels 'a sense sublime / Of something far more deeply interfused'. The 'sense sublime', poetically inverting noun and adjective, might threaten to fly off into improbability were it not tied down by the humble vagueness of 'something'. 'Interfused' is unusual, but perfectly suggests how generally and deeply hidden the 'presence' is. But Wordsworth must say more, and he does so triumphantly, with a collection of startling and original **epithets** and **metaphors** for general aspects of nature. The presence's 'dwelling' is 'the light of setting suns', a striking movement from a relatively ordinary, nearly concrete word to an abstract and impossible conception. Equally, in what ways is the ocean 'round' and the air 'living'? Explanations can of course be found, but these are still thrillingly odd adjectives, creating a new way of thinking about the elemental ocean and air. In the next line 'the blue sky' (no need now to go beyond the obvious cliché; too many verbal fireworks might alienate the reader), image of huge emptiness, is in conjunction with 'the mind of man', perhaps the most surprising dwelling place for this 'presence', bringing the conception down to earth, yet its discovery in humanity is the climax of the argument.

Wordsworth now tells us about the 'presence'. It is a 'motion' and a 'spirit' – the one a matter of physics, the other divinity. It 'impels', a strong active verb. And what it impels is all 'thinking things', bringing together the human capacity for thought with the *thinginess* of existence, and 'all objects of all thought'. And now Wordsworth has to find a verb to bring to life his idea of an energy propelling absolutely everything in the world (the word 'all' appears four times in these two lines). The 'motion' and 'spirit' '*rolls through* all things'; what a strange and effective concept is created by this choice of words. 'Rolls' is a pleasantly concrete verb, in contrast with 'impels'; it seems relaxed, ordinary and gentle. It brilliantly concludes a difficult passage, one that might have repelled readers by high-flown abstraction were it not constantly tied down by Wordsworth's exact and surprising word-choice.

Poetry for comparison: *The Prelude*, Book XI, lines 258–345, (pp. 213–15)

101 **interfused** blended together

114 **genial spirits** to do with genius; poetic perception and inspiration

'THERE WAS A BOY'

FROM *LYRICAL BALLADS*, 1800 (pp. 126–7; this poem also appears in Book V of *The Prelude*)

Making owls hoot and the aftermath

There was a boy who lived near a lake. Often in the evening he used to make hooting noises, to make the owls reply. He would really get them going, hooting like mad. Sometimes, however, they would not reply, and in the silence, while he was listening in expectation, he would suddenly be surprised by the sound of the streams, or the scenery, the rocks, the woods and the lake. This imagery would enter his heart and mind without his knowing it.

It is a beautiful area, where he lived, and often I think I have stood near his grave, for he died when he was only ten.

> This is another example of Wordsworth's exercising his skill with blank verse. It consists of a single moment in the life of a country boy. What is notable in this passage is the way the poet depicts the boy in the countryside. We are told the cliffs of Winander knew the boy, reversing the more usual logic that the boy should know the cliffs, and establishing the idea that boy and countryside are inextricably connected. The sense of exactly how the boy held his hands to make owl noises helps us to empathise with him: we enter his consciousness. The verse enacts the 'wild scene' (line 15) of boy and owls hooting at each other. This clamour is followed by the surprise of silence, which is emphasised by repetition, and underlined by alliterative sibilants. The 'gentle shock' and 'mild surprise' (line 19) is another repetition for emphasis, in this case double, as both adjectives and nouns are parallel. Nature is actively responding to the boy. First the owls make their reply, but the silence mocks his skill, the 'voice of mountain torrents' (line 21) enters his heart, and the 'visible scene' (line 21) enters 'unawares into his mind' (line 22). 'Unawares' is syntactically floating: does it apply to him or the scenery? Finally the 'solemn imagery' (line 23) of the rocks and woods and sky is received 'into the bosom' not as we expect of the

boy, but 'of the steady lake' (line 25). It turns into an image of reflection, yet it reinforces the way in which nature is anthropomorphised, while the boy has all but ceased to exist except in terms of the solemn natural imagery which surrounds him.

This poem also provides an example of an aspect of consciousness that seems to have fascinated Wordsworth, and which often features in *The Prelude*. When the mind concentrates hard on one thing (calling up the owls), and then that activity is stopped, the mind's concentration is transferred unawares to something else (the surrounding scenery).

Poetry for comparison: *The Prelude*, Book I, lines 372–427, and 452–489, pp. 11–14

5 **rising or setting** this refers to the stars, but grammatically it could also apply to the hills, or even the boy. The syntax is fluid

16 **jocund** joyful

'STRANGE FITS OF PASSION'   FROM *LYRICAL BALLADS*, 1800 (pp. 127–8)

A lover's odd perception of the moon

I have experienced 'strange fits of passion' (line 1). I would only dare tell other people who have been in love what happened to me once. Once when the woman I loved was in her prime I made my way to her cottage. The moon was overhead in the evening sky. I looked at the moon as I rode my horse towards those paths which I knew so well. Eventually I reached the orchard and hill where the cottage was, and as I climbed the hill, the moon seemed to descend in the sky. I was in a kind of dream or trance, almost half asleep, watching the moon. My horse walked steadily on. Suddenly the moon appeared to drop behind the cottage roof. At this moment a peculiar thought of the kind that occurs to lovers slid into my head: 'What if Lucy should be dead!' (line 28).

This poem offers a strange little story to illustrate the odd processes of human consciousness, especially in the psyches of those who are in love. It describes an intimation of the death of a loved one.

This is one of the so-called 'Lucy poems', about which there has been much biographical and psychological speculation, none of it conclusive. In these poems Wordsworth seems to have wanted to imagine what it would be like to feel grief at the death of someone he loved, a process not that different from adopting the other masks or **personae** that he uses in some of *Lyrical Ballads*. We might also wonder if the Lucy poems refer obliquely to some part of himself which he felt he had lost. Though Wordsworth was still relatively young when he was writing *Lyrical Ballads*, poems like 'Tintern Abbey' (written when he was twenty-eight) are filled with a sense of loss that the 'aching joys' and 'dizzy raptures' of childhood are no more. Perhaps these poems stand as symbols of human grief and loss, not necessarily located in anything the poet experienced. Certainly 'Strange fits of Passion' seeks to generalise the experience it describes, as only comprehensible to the community of those who have been in love. And it is told as a bare, somewhat contorted, narrative, and not a personal meditation. The language is occasionally stilted, with poetic **inversions** that sometimes make the syntax initially a little difficult to unravel:

> And I will dare to tell,
> But in the lover's ear alone,
> What once to me befell.
> When she I loved ... (lines 2–5)

This may be ascribed to the awkwardness of confessing such an apparently trivial and neurotic incident.

At the centre of the poem is an optical illusion like that which occurs during the boat-stealing episode in *The Prelude* (see pp. 59, 63). As he rides uphill towards the cottage, the roof of the cottage suddenly comes between him and the moon, at which he has been dreamily staring. Till this moment it has appeared to be steadily 'descending' (line 19) but then its disappearance is as if the planet 'dropped' (line 24) behind the cottage roof. At the surprise of this loss, the possibility of another more grievous disappearance pops into the narrator's mind. What might have been no more than a quirky psychological aberration is given a prophetic meaning by the fact that the other Lucy poems are epitaphs for someone who has died.

The moon is a traditional symbol of change, waxing and waning as it does through its monthly cycle. Wordsworth's moon is peculiarly fixed in the intensity of the narrator's gaze while he rides; but it is also oddly mobile, as it seems to descend and drop with uncanny speed, made strange by the optical illusion described above.

Poem for comparison: 'Louisa' (p. 279)

SONG ('SHE DWELT AMONG TH' UNTRODDEN WAYS')
FROM *LYRICAL BALLADS*, 1800 (p. 128)

Epitaph for Lucy

This short lyric consists of a number of comments and descriptive metaphors about a young woman who was known to the speaker and has died.

Wordsworth achieves an effect of mysteriousness in this poem by putting together a number of statements that contradict each other, or which deny a clear interpretation. How could the 'ways' where Lucy dwelt be 'untrodden' (line 1)? If there was 'none to praise' her, how could there be 'very few to love' (lines 3–4)? If she lived 'unknown' how could 'few' (line 9) know that she had died? It is possible to force a logic from these contradictions – for example, 'unknown' could simply mean that she was not famous, rather than completely devoid of human companionship; the paths near her dwelling place might be relatively, not absolutely 'untrodden'. However, to insist upon this kind of reading would be to miss the overall effect of the poem, which is to suggest the powerlessness of language to pin down the nature of Lucy's ethereal existence, almost as if she was some kind of wood spirit or nymph, and at the end of the poem, the poet's inability to put his grief into words. 'And, oh! / The difference to me' (lines 11–12) is a line which blankly and obliquely refers to a depth of feeling which it is incapable of expressing. It is beyond poetic means, ineffable, indescribable.

In the middle verse there are two strange metaphors, where once again the poet seems to make a statement which he then qualifies in a way that provokes a sense of mystery. She is 'a violet by a mossy stone' (line 5), but 'half-hidden from the eye' (line 6); the first image provides clarity, solidity and colour, but this is immediately blurred by what follows; what is given is quickly taken away. Equally the next image starts with a simple statement. She is as 'fair as a star', yet this is 'when only one / Is shining in the sky' (lines 7 and 8). This extension does not render the image vague, rather it makes it sharper, but its effect is still odd; it implies that Lucy is single, unique, incomparable, remote, and even perhaps hints at her loneliness.

Poem for comparison: 'Lucy Gray' (pp. 130–2)

A SLUMBER DID MY SPIRIT SEAL   FROM *LYRICAL BALLADS*, 1800 (p. 129)

Another Lucy epitaph

I was wrapped in sleep, and did not imagine that Lucy existed in a world of time and age. Now she is dead, and the only life that she has is that of the natural world.

It is extraordinary that Wordsworth's range as a poet extends from the meditative blank verse of 'Tintern Abbey', to a jewel-like lyric such as this poem. Once more his words gain their peculiar power from contradictions, which in this case produce a pattern of inscrutable ambiguity that resonates well beyond the apparent limits of a tiny verse consisting of no more than two sentences and eight short lines. Interestingly Wordsworth uses some of his odd word-choices – 'thing', 'motion', 'force' and 'roll' (second stanza) – that occur in the long meditation, where they have a context and meaning that is both similar and, perhaps, quite different.

The memorable first line, with its three words beginning with 's', introduces the idea of sleep and a distant and disengaged numbness; the poet describes his spirit as *sealed*, wrapped away and cut off from what? From human fears; a strange idea, and desirable? The qualification that follows is initially equally puzzling. 'She', the subject of the poem, never mentioned by name, formerly seemed 'a thing' – a strange word for a loved-one – but her thing-like quality, we learn, is because she was imagined by him, in his slumber, to be outside and beyond the processes of aging and time, 'the touch of earthly years' (first stanza). In other words she seemed to him outside earth-bound humanity, some kind of spirit.

This person now has no 'motion' or 'force'. Death has deprived her of her human senses of sight and hearing. But she is still in some kind of movement; she is 'rolled round' (line 7) in the daily motion of the earth with other natural objects, with rocks and stones (utterly dead) and with trees (alive, and subject to growth and time, but not human, or even animal). 'Earth' (line 7) hints at the grave, as well as referring to the celestial body that rolls through space. She is now a 'thing' (line 3) indeed, making us realise the full irony of the first stanza. It is she now who slumbers, who is sealed away in death, who is beyond human fears because she has succumbed to a source of human fear, death. Whereas before she seemed insulated from the touch of time, now she is indeed separated from all 'touch' (line 4) and feeling. The poet however has woken from his slumber to find all that he should have feared has come to pass.

How is the reader supposed to feel about the absoluteness of death as described in the poem? Is the motion she has now – anonymous, geological, natural, and astronomical – supposed to make us feel better about death, or is it a confession that the natural world is indeed utterly dead, not the active environment for human perception for which Wordsworth argues in so many poems. This is the huge ambiguity of feeling with which the poem must leave the reader.

Poem for comparison: 'Surprised by joy, impatient as the wind' (p. 323)

7 **diurnal** daily

MICHAEL: A PASTORAL POEM   FROM *LYRICAL BALLADS,* 1800 (pp. 154–66)

A sad tale of a shepherd's life

In the mountains there is a hidden valley, where you can be alone. The following story is about a heap of stones that can be found there. It is a demonstration of the poet's beliefs about shepherds and 'the heart of man'

y

(line 33). Once there was a shepherd called Michael who lived near Grasmere. He was unusually strong and hardworking, and eighty years old. He loved the countryside in which he worked. He lived with his wife and son, and his two sheep-dogs. The family was famous locally for its hard work. Michael was devoted to his son, Luke, now eighteen, and had often looked after him as a baby and a small boy.

Bad news comes to the household: Michael had acted as surety for his nephew, things have gone wrong, and now he has to pay this money, which amounts to half his savings. First he thinks he will sell land, but having worked so hard to buy it, he cannot do this. He comes up with the plan of sending Luke to work with a tradesman in town. Luke can quickly earn the money, and the entire property will be his to inherit. Isabel, Michael's wife, reluctantly agrees to this idea.

Michael was intending to build a sheep-fold up in the valley mentioned at the start of the poem, and he walks up there with Luke. He tells his son how much he loves him, looking back on the boy's childhood, and Luke is moved. He asks Luke to lay the first stone of the sheep-fold, and wants him to think of this when he is in the town, as an emblem of his family's way of life.

To begin with they hear good news of Luke's success in his work, but soon he takes up dissolute city ways, and eventually has to escape overseas. Michael continues to visit the valley for the remaining seven years before he dies, but he never builds the sheep-fold. Isabel dies soon after him, their house is sold, and nothing of it any longer remains, except for a nearby tree, and the heap of stones up in the valley.

> 'Michael' is an unusually straightforward narrative poem and is much admired for the directness and simplicity of its style. It demonstrates how the human story can be read even in an apparently bare landscape; it gives meaning to a heap of stones. Everything leads forwards to explaining the dreadful pathos of the famous line: 'And never lifted up a single stone' (line 475). 'Michael' is also a demonstration of the ideas Wordsworth put forward in the 'Preface' to the second edition of *Lyrical Ballads*, about 'humble and rustic life' and 'the essential passions of the heart' (see pp. 103–6) and indeed in the second verse paragraph of the poem, the narrator restates these views for the purposes of the poem.

The subtitle 'pastoral' is wryly ironic: Michael is not a pipe-playing artificial figure of pastoral poetry, but a wind-burnt, practical man, dedicated to his flock in all weathers. He and his wife work hard to improve their property and position – she by her spinning, he by unstinting toil and thrift. If 'Michael' is Wordsworth's attempt to show the dignity of labour, then there is not actually a great deal of information about the working practices of shepherds other than in incidental details, such as Luke as a small boy annoying the sheep during shearing. And these details are aimed also at showing the old man's special fondness for his only son. This love – and its terrible disappointment – is the one of the 'essential passions of the heart' at the centre of the poem, as specified by Wordsworth in his 'Preface'.

And the end of the poem Michael's way of life has been swept away. Suddenly the tale seems to have happened long ago. Wordsworth's readers would have known that the days of spinning as a cottage industry had passed. Is this a nostalgic, even a sentimental tale, harking back to a former age? In spite of the dignified plainness of Michael's life and Wordsworth's re-telling of it, is there something oppressive about the biblical covenant that the old man makes with his son, concerning the heap of stones? Is Wordsworth saying that such disappointment and sorrow is inevitable, that no amount of thrift and hard work to shore up the future can save us from the tragedies of loss, disillusionment and death?

Poetry for comparison: 'The Ruined Cottage' (pp. 39–53); *The Prelude*, Book VIII, lines 222–311, 312–428 (pp. 132–37)

R ESOLUTION AND INDEPENDENCE, ORIGINALLY CALLED 'THE LEECH-GATHERER'   FROM *POEMS IN TWO VOLUMES*, 1807: VOLUME 1 (pp. 287–91)

Wisdom of an old man encountered on the moor

After a storm the natural world is bright and new, with sunshine illuminating the wet countryside. Birds and animals seem to be finding joy in the good weather, especially a hare running through the wet grass, raising a spray of mist that follows her. The poet is walking on the moor, and feels the burden of his melancholy memories lifted from him. But then, just as quickly, he finds himself plunged into a terrible dejection. He sees the creatures enjoying the sunshine, and knows he should be like them, but cannot escape the fear that dreadful things may befall him. He worries that he has not taken heed of what may happen. He thinks of other poets who have died in misery and poverty, and decides that poets usually start out happy, but descend into despondency and madness.

Suddenly – perhaps it was divine intervention – he comes upon an old man; he seems to be the oldest man he has ever seen. The poet watches him standing by a pond. Like a rock or some kind of sea-beast that has crawled from the sea, this old man looks only half human, neither quite alive nor dead. He is bent almost double, propped up on a staff, standing motionless by the pond. With his staff he stirs the pond, looking into it as intently as if he was reading a book. The poet engages him in conversation, finally asking what he is doing in such a lonely spot. The man replies, solemnly and carefully, that he makes his living by going from pool to pool on the moors looking for leeches. The poet loses a sense of what the man is saying, and starts to think of him as something in a dream, sent to give him strength. All the dreadful impending miseries and fears return, and in anguish he asks the old man again, how does he live? What does he do? The old man explains again that he travels the moors gathering leeches, but whereas there used to be plenty, now their numbers are dwindling. The poet imagines the old man wandering unceasingly around the moor. Once more the old man explains what he is doing, and then moves on to other topics. Suddenly the poet realises the folly of his questions, and how firm in mind the old man is, in spite of his decrepit body, and resolves that when looking for help in the future, he will think of the leech-gatherer on the lonely moor.

This poem exhibits some of Wordsworth's best qualities as a poet, and, perhaps, some of his faults, though these are also peculiarly his own, and may be redeemed if the reader decides that the poem's possibly comic aspect is deliberate, and not a by-product of the poet's solemnity and lack of self-knowledge. Its preoccupations are typically Wordsworthian: the poet plunges from joyful celebration of the beautiful morning to abject gloom. He seems to have no capacity to control this wild fluctuation in his mood, which he ascribes to his status as a poet, for whom the inevitable parabola seems to be towards despair and madness. He sees the old man as an agent from another world, who has the secret of right living and repeatedly – and comically? – asks him for the secret of life. The poor old chap patiently explains three times that he is a leech-gatherer, until Wordsworth is laughingly brought to his senses.

Some of the language is ploddingly exact. Coleridge (in Chapter XXII of the *Biographia Literaria* published in 1817) saw part of the ninth stanza (lines 59–63) as irredeemably prosaic and an example of Wordsworth's unevenness as a poet. Half the stanza will suffice:

> My course I stopped as soon as I espied
> The old man in that naked wilderness:
> Close by a pond, upon the further side,
> He stood alone. (lines 57–60)

There is a plonking exactitude in this – Coleridge's term is '*matter-of-factness*' – though the 'naked' wilderness is an example of figurative language, rendering the landscape human, which links in with other metaphors throughout the poem.

Early on there is a gem-like description of a hare racing through the sunlit, wet grass:

> The hare is running races in her mirth,
> And with her feet she from the plashy earth
> Raises a mist, which glittering in the sun,
> Runs with her all the way, wherever she doth run. (lines 11–14)

First this anthropomorphises the animal, ascribing to it the human capacity for mirth, and then the mist itself is animated, so that it runs races with the hare.

The later description of the old man works in the opposite direction, turning him by metaphor into a strange conjunction of rock and sea creature, 'not all alive nor dead' (line 71). Wordsworth himself uses this stanza as an example of how the imagination works in his 1815 'Preface' to the poems. What is particularly striking about this long **simile**, which extends over seven lines, is that it almost seems to work backwards. It starts with the stone – the **vehicle** of the metaphor; the simile's **tenor** (the old man) is delayed till the start of the next stanza. All who see it 'couched on the bald top of an eminence' (line 65) ('couched' is a word with oddly comfortable connotations) wonder how it got there, so that it seems 'a thing endued with sense' (line 68), and then, a simile within the simile, the rock is compared to a sea-beast – a seal or walrus perhaps – that has crawled out of the water, to sun itself on a rock or sand. The next stanza ties up the threefold comparison – 'Such seemed, this man' (line 71). A rock is like a sea-beast which is like the old man: there is a complex relationship here between the animal, the inanimate and the human, parallel in kind but different from the hare-human and mist of the second stanza.

These metaphorical linkages between the world of things, animals and humans are at the heart of the poem's argument. It is poets, quintessentially, perhaps exaggeratedly human in their capacity to feel, that are burdened by the capacity to think of misery in the midst of joy; an interesting exercise is to count up the number of examples of 'the ways of men, so vain and melancholy' (line 21) which the poet lists throughout the poem. Birds do their singing when the sun shines after a storm; an aged leech-gatherer continues with his business of prodding his stick into ponds. But the poet, imagining beyond the sufficiency of the present place and moment, has to be laughed back to reality. The old man is a rebuke to the narrator for his oneness with nature – the kind of country dweller that Wordsworth extols as the proper subject for poetry at several points in *The Prelude*. This is an imagined sage, perhaps even a wizard with his wand, who triumphantly changes into a perfectly ordinary old man, and his ordinariness teaches the poet more of a lesson about 'Resolution and Independence' than he could possibly have derived from his neurotic and inappropriate metaphysical questions. We are left wondering whether or not Wordsworth wants us to laugh at his narrator's sudden return to common sense.

Wordsworth employs an unusual seven-line stanza in this poem. Six lines of iambic pentameter are followed by a single line of hexameter. The rhyme scheme – *ababbcc* – creates interesting relationships between the parts of the poem, with the final three lines tied to the opening quatrain (*abab*) by a linking rhyme, and the last two lines coming together as an uneven couplet, with its trailing long second line threatening to break apart. This is highly patterned but asymmetric verse, creating just the right kind of wobbly mixture of order and disorder for Wordsworth's account of abject dejection on a sunny day.

Poems for comparison: *The Pedlar*; 'Old Man Travelling'; 'The Old Cumberland Beggar' (pp. 54, 109, 144); *The Prelude*, Book IV, 363–463 (pp. 63–66)

42 **Chatterton** Thomas Chatterton (1752–70) invented a whole corpus of fake medieval poetry under the name of Sir Thomas Rowley; he committed suicide at the age of seventeen

45–6 **Of him who walked in glory and in joy / Behind his plough** Robert Burns (1759–96), Scottish, the so-called 'ploughman poet', who was a farm labourer, till he published his poetry. Eventually he became a customs official. He was much more successful as a poet than as a farmer

107 **leech** a parasitic worm that sucks blood from mammals, used by doctors in the past (and still occasionally nowadays) to draw blood from a patient as a cure

Composed upon Westminster Bridge
FROM *POEMS IN TWO VOLUMES*, 1807: VOLUME 1 (p. 294)

A beautiful cityscape

The poet takes pleasure in a panorama of London with its buildings and surrounding countryside in the calm of an early morning.

London, described without sympathy in Book VII of *The Prelude*, in this sonnet is transformed by metaphor into 'a sight so touching in its majesty' (line 3). The city is connected immediately to the 'Earth', which is the first word of the poem. It is then humanised: it wears 'the beauty of the morning' (line 5) like a garment. Paradoxically we are then told that its 'ships, towers, domes, theatres and temples' (line 6) – concrete items which make up the more abstract idea of the city – are 'bare' (line 5), and lie 'open unto the fields and to the sky' (line 7),

y

bringing the city and fields into an unexpected proximity with the countryside (though in 1803 the area around Westminster Bridge would undoubtedly have been more rural than it is now). The air is smokeless. So far the city is being defined through the opposite of its stereotypical attributes. It is 'silent' (line 5), countrified, peaceful, and without people; its buildings are 'bright and glittering' (line 8). Indeed, it is more beautiful than the country:

> Never did sun more beautifully steep
> In his first splendour valley, rock, or hill. (lines 9–10)

The poet asserts he has never seen or felt 'a calm so deep' (line 11). Under the bridge, a humanised river 'glideth at his own sweet will' (line 13), and the houses are asleep. All is anthropomorphised. Indeed the 'mighty heart' (line 14) of the city is lying still: is it even dead, perhaps?

A city seen from such a perversely non-urban perspective is a kind of triumph, though of course cities have their moments of peace and sunlight. The poem satisfies by turning all our expectations about London upside down, excluding any reference to humanity except through the persistent humanising of its non-human elements, and by metaphor creating a visionary picture.

Poem for contrast: *The Prelude*, Book VIII, lines 589–623 (pp. 246–7)

THE SOLITARY REAPER   FROM *POEMS IN TWO VOLUMES*, 1807: VOLUME 2 (p. 301)

A melancholy song examined

The poet comes across a young Highland woman, on her own, reaping and singing. He is entranced by her song, and wonders what it is about. Long after he can no longer hear it, it remains in his mind.

> The title announces the subject of the poem, and this is also spelled out clearly in the first stanza. The poet comes across a young woman working in the fields, who is singing as she reaps and binds the grain (it is thus late summer). The girl's melancholy song is turned by metaphor into a liquid, which fills the valley so that it overflows.

The second stanza contains two little scenes by which the poet explains how welcome and refreshing the music is to him. The first conjures up a moment in the desert – the Arabian sands – when travellers are resting at an oasis and a nightingale sings to them. The second evokes the cuckoo singing over the sea in the farthest Hebrides. Though both these **vignettes** are offered as analogies to the girl's song, they are markedly in contrast to each other. The first involves an exotic location, the desert, which generally stands for dryness and sterility, though here it is the backdrop for a companionable moment – a band of travellers rest gratefully in the shade. The second brings the poem back to Scotland, the Outer Hebrides being the extreme north-west point in the British Isles. The cuckoo – a bird of the woods heralding the spring, and not associated with the ocean – is 'breaking the silence' (line 15) of the seas. Seas do not normally stand for silence: the poem starts to move in a peculiar and unexpected direction. The ideas which compose this second image – cuckoo, sea, silence – are brought together in unexpected ways. There are no people who might enjoy the bird's song. The cuckoo seems to be singing to itself alone and the silent seas, and the final impression left by the scene is one of eerie emptiness and solitude. This lonely barrenness contrasts with the nightingale's refreshing song. The reader is reminded of the solitariness of the reaper.

Wordsworth asks what she is singing about. But this is a **rhetorical question,** and he provides two possible answers himself, and as in the second stanza, these two answers are in contrast with each other. The first suggestion is that the 'plaintive numbers flow' (line 18) (taking up the image of the song as water) for old stories, tales of battles and public events that happened long ago – this evokes the world of the Scottish ballads. The second suggestion is that she sings about some ordinary private family matter, 'some natural sorrow, loss or pain / That has been and may be again' (lines 23–4). Wordsworth here makes 'natural' his list of possible miseries, and the fact that they are likely to be repeated. The reader is made to share in his pessimism.

Finally he returns to the Highland lass herself, though he says little about her, except that she is working hard, and her song continues.

We may infer from this that she has not seen the poet, and he has not spoken to her. Long after he can no longer hear her, he remembers her song. A strange shift has occurred: the first three stanzas are in the present tense, while here the poem moves into the past, so that the events of the poem are suddenly thrust back into the past, and 'long after it was heard no more' (line 32) suggests far more time may have elapsed than the few minutes taken to pass beyond hearing distance – the poet seems to be remembering her far back in time. The reader may wonder how far he has progressed on life's journey, not just the weary hill up which he 'mounted' (line 30) after leaving her.

'Will no one tell me what she sings?' asks the poet in the third stanza. 'Behold', 'Stop here, or gently pass', 'Listen' (first stanza): the poem starts with a number of requests and addresses to an imaginary person. And yet these are clearly rhetorical gestures, the kind of things that are said in the strange and imaginary world of poems. It is the reader who must obey these imperatives, and thereby is involved in the poet's intimate monologue. The over-riding impression is that the poet is alone. This is the result of a number of suggestions. First of all, we are told tautologically in the title and in the poem how solitary the reaper is: she is also 'single', 'by herself' and 'alone' (first stanza). The speaker is so struck by her solitariness, that we come to associate it with him, as we do also the image of the lonely cuckoo, and the assumptions that loss and pain are 'natural' (line 23). The poet refers to himself for the first time in the last stanza and it is a single 'I' who saw the young woman, who listened, and who continued on his apparently exhausting journey, and who carried the memory of her song in his heart. Memory is private and internal, though here it has been shared. We cannot but draw the conclusion that the poem is about the poet rather than the reaper herself, or if it is not about the poet, since we learn little about him except his frame of mind, then it consists of his reaction to the reaper. There is, after all, no description of the young woman at all. The sum total of what we know about her is that she is 'reaping and singing by herself' (line 3). The poem is an imaginative reverie around this fact.

The poem is not a study of the dignity of labour, and nor is it a thesis on the behaviour of birds. We may wonder whether nightingales sing in Arabian oases and the cuckoo over the Hebridean seas. These birds and their songs are also a typical property of poetry. The nightingale, the bird that sings alone in the night, is a traditional symbol of poetry itself. If the poem is neither about the reaper, nor the birds, it is most emphatically about song – considerations of song appear in every stanza. Her song is melancholy, and sung as it is in Gaelic, its subject has to be guessed at by the poet. Yet it is consoling and refreshing to the poet, who listens till he has had his fill, and then carries it in his heart for future restoration. This is one of the paradoxes at the heart of poetry itself: we may read a poem entirely sad in its emphasis, but be charmed, consoled and cheered by it. It is the nature of song to confront 'sorrow, loss, and pain' (line 23) and by turning it into 'numbers', ordering it into melodies, patterns in sound, making it beautiful and therefore acceptable. And poetry (or at least this kind of poetry) works in just the same way, dealing with human misery, and by heightening the language in which it written – by metre, metaphor and other figurative aspects of language – rendering that misery beautiful and therefore consoling. So just as the solitary reaper by her song finds a way of coping with the vicissitudes of human life, so Wordsworth has done the same for us in his poem 'The Solitary Reaper', taking his own aloneness and making of it a highly symmetrical and satisfying pattern in words and ideas that seeks to console our own melancholy – we also can take away the memory of his music. This poem, then, offers a kind of simple theory and demonstration of what art can do for us.

The poem's success relies, as do many of Wordsworth's poems, on its apparent authenticity, its candour, its transparent sincerity. It reads like something that actually happened to the poet; it deals with 'real' things: or so it seems. 'The Solitary Reaper', through Wordsworth's skill, achieves an admirable sense of authenticity. Ironically – and this does not deter in any way from its excellence – it grows out of Wordsworth's reading, and not his experience. It is built out of an incident related in Thomas Wilkinson's *Tour in Scotland*:

> Passed a female who was reaping alone; she sung in Erse, as she bended
> over her sickle; the sweetest voice I ever heard: her strains were tenderly
> melancholy, and felt delicious, long after they were heard no more.

This graceful little poem consists of four eight-line stanzas each one rhymed *ababccdd* so that metrically each stanza falls naturally into two quatrains, one with interlaced rhyme and one consisting of two couplets. The poem's grammar follows this metrical arrangement, with each stanza falling into two separate units of sense. So it is very highly symmetrical and carefully ordered; but in spite of being so highly patterned, and though it contains the occasional poetic inversion for the sake of the rhyme ('the vale profound', line 7), it still reads as if the language was perfectly natural, simple and relaxed. Wordsworth seems to arrive at such a verbal symmetry without any strain.

Poem for comparison: 'Stepping Westward' (p. 302); 'To the Cuckoo', (p. 306); Keats: 'Ode to a Nightingale'

M Y HEART LEAPS UP   FROM *POEMS IN TWO VOLUMES*, 1807: VOLUME 2 (p. 305)

Natural piety

The poet expresses pleasure at seeing a rainbow, something that has remained consistent since childhood, and he hopes will last into old age. He wants his life to be bound together by this natural piety.

A simple poem about Wordsworth's attitude to nature, this requires little explication but some comment. In spite of its simplicity, at its centre there is a pleasantly paradoxical statement – the idea that the child is 'father' (line 7) of the man (meaning that adult ideas and habits grow out of childhood experience) – which has become proverbial.

The choice of a rainbow as the symbolic natural event to which Wordsworth ties his faith in nature is interesting. After the Flood, God sent the rainbow as a covenant to Noah that such a thing would not happen again (Genesis 3: 13). In his *Optics* (1704) Newton provided a scientific explanation for the rainbow which was a model for empirical scientific investigation during the eighteenth century. So Wordsworth has chosen to focus on a phenomenon that has symbolic significance from both a religious and a scientific point of view, and uses it to express his own version of religion, 'natural piety' (line 8), based on day-to-day respect and love for the things of Nature, which he believes has given his life a coherence and consistency that he hopes will continue. In a mild rebuff to science, Wordsworth implicitly evaluates simple joy at the colours of the rainbow before rational, scientific analysis.

Poem for comparison: 'Ode: Intimations of Immortality' (pp. 314–19)

'I WANDERED LONELY AS A CLOUD'
FROM *POEMS IN TWO VOLUMES*, 1807: VOLUME 2 (p. 306)

Daffodils seen and remembered

While wandering in the countryside the poet came across masses of daffodils growing by a lake. The sight was immensely cheering, but he could not know how pleasing the memory of the daffodils would be to him in the future.

This is Wordsworth's most well known poem, and has appeared in anthologies of all kinds as a typical example of his work. It is often cited as an example of all that is sentimental and superficial about his poetry. The cultural specificity of its subject matter has caused irritation. Readers from, for example, Australia or Africa, are often alienated by a poem presented to them as by a 'great' writer, but which extols the beauties of a North European flower unknown in their own landscape. However in one respect it is not typically Wordsworthian: it is unusually sunny, with no references to death and despondency, present, past or impending – the 'vacant or pensive mood' (line 14) is a relatively mild contrast to the joyful sight of the daffodils, and even this is connected with 'the bliss of solitude' (line 16).

The cross-over metaphors between the human and inanimate world are entirely typical. The poet is turned into a cloud, as an example of

y

loneliness. We may wonder why clouds are perceived by Wordsworth as particularly lonely, unless it is to do with their loftiness in relation to the 'vales and hills' (line 2). On the other hand the flowers are instantly figured by means of human qualities: they are a crowd or host – both collective nouns more commonly used of people – and they are dancing. So are the waves of the lake, even more gleefully. Feelings are ascribed to these objects, which are 'a laughing company' (line 10). There is an inherent opposition between the poet's solitariness and the companionable multiplicity of flowers and waves.

This poem is a singular demonstration of Wordsworth's definition of poetry in the 'Preface to the Lyrical Ballads' as 'emotion recollected in tranquillity', a formula that applies both to the composition of the verse, and the pattern of the poem's 'argument' about the restorative effect of a remembered moment, as in *The Prelude*. The 'inward eye / Which is the bliss of solitude' (lines 15–16) returns to the idea of loneliness with which the poem began, though here the idea of being alone is introduced oddly in relation to 'bliss' (line 16). But the poem finishes in unequivocally cheerful tone, the poet's heart filling with pleasure and dancing with the flowers.

Poem for contrast: 'Steamboats, Viaducts, and Railways' (p. 371)

ODE (THERE WAS A TIME – ODE: INTIMATIONS OF IMMORTALITY FROM RECOLLECTIONS OF EARLY CHILDHOOD); (hereafter called 'The Immortality Ode') FROM *POEMS IN TWO VOLUMES*, 1807: VOLUME 2 (pp. 314–19)

Youth's joyful vision lost, with some recompense

There was a time for the poet when everything in the world seemed glorious and fresh, but now he can no longer see things in this way. Everything – the rainbow, the moon, flowers, water, sunshine – is just as beautiful as it was, but some glory has been lost.

Now, while the birds and lambs are enjoying spring, a sense of misery has overcome him, but he has put it into words and felt relief. He is determined that his grief will not spoil this joyful May morning, which all Nature seems to be celebrating: let the shepherd boys shout! He feels the festivity of all creatures around him. How could he be sullen on such a day, when children are enjoying the sunshine on every side? He can hear their joy. But still he can see a single tree, a field, a flower, and they tell him that something has gone: what has happened to the sense of dreamlike glory which he used to feel?

Life is just a short sleep for the soul, which is immortal, existing both before and after our mortal life. We come from God, and in infancy we still have knowledge of that Heaven. As we grow older, through childhood and youth, this bright vision grows weaker, until in adulthood it fades into the light of common day.

The world, like a mother with a foster child, tries to distract us from remembering the beautiful place from which we came. If you watch small children playing in front of their proud parents, you will see that they spend all their time like little actors pretending to be adults, filling their imaginary stage with imitations of people of all ages.

But the appearance of small children belies their true worth. They are huge of soul; they are philosophers, prophets, seers. They possess truths which adults toil to understand. They know that they are immortal, and that the grave is just a cold bed where we wait for something else. Why is it then that children, while at their most glorious, spend their time provoking age to come upon them? The burdens of adulthood will weigh upon them soon enough.

At least it is a pleasure to remember what we have lost. The memory of childhood is blessed. Not for its simple delights and freedom does the poet give thanks, but for moments of questioning and bewilderment, misgivings and fears, and first affections and dim recollection. It is these that shed light on everything that we do, and give us help and solace. These offer unperishable truths that nothing we can do can spoil, and from which we can always maintain a distant sense of our immortality.

So, let the birds sing and the lambs jump. We can join in, even though nothing can quite bring back the glorious vision that we used to feel. We can find strength in what we have been left, sympathy, faith and mature philosophy.

The poet states that he has not fallen out of love with the natural world that surrounds him, though he has lost the delight of being constantly in its power. He still finds the brooks and dawning sunshine beautiful. He can now see the sunset with an eye made more mature by the knowledge of mortality. Things are different; but thanks to the capacity for human feeling, even a mere flower can provide the poet with profound and moving ideas.

In 1815 Wordsworth used the last three lines of 'My heart leaps up' (p. 305) as the epigraph of this Ode, which expands the idea that 'the child is father of the man' to the point of hyperbole, and offers a less assured definition of 'natural piety', in terms of the great losses and small rewards of maturity.

This is a difficult poem, full of abstractions and ideas that are both difficult to grasp from the way Wordsworth has expressed them, and tenuous. A rough summary of the poem's argument makes the poem sound peculiarly bare, because it dredges out all the figurative language, and yet this is a work exceptionally rich in wonderful metaphorical phraseology. The situation of the poem is a sunny spring day in the countryside, surrounded by lambs and children, but this is not a description of a particular moment, a 'spot of time'. It is more the pastoral landscape of the poetic imagination, an artificial world where the shepherd boys play tabors and pipes, and pick flowers in 'a thousand valleys' (line 47), harking back to the Greek and Roman poets who initiated this kind of writing. Words describing the day – 'festival', 'coronal' and 'jubilee' (lines 37–40) – also suggest this artificiality. And the language Wordsworth employs is not designed to picture an authentic scene, but to deal with the ideas that concern him – the loss of that glorious vision that he felt in his childhood perception of the natural world. The characteristic method of the poem is to link an abstraction with something more concrete, resulting in many vivid and memorable phrases. Here are some examples from the first third of the poem, mixing abstraction and concretion in this way:

'The sunshine is a glorious birth' (line 16)
'The winds come to me from the fields of sleep' (line 28)
'Thou child of joy' (line 34)
'Whither is fled the visionary dream?' (line 56)
'Our birth is but a sleep and a forgetting' (line 58)
'The soul that rises with us, our life's star' (line 59)
'But trailing clouds of glory do we come' (line 64)

Such a list can be made for the whole poem, and provides a useful key to its methods and Wordsworth's skill as a poet. In this work he seems to aim at an aphoristic style quite unlike the simplicity of many of his early verses.

In general the simple objects of nature are dignified and made special by the metaphor. What for example are 'the fields of sleep' (line 28)? The phrase is rich with possibilities, but without precise meaning. What is 'the hour / Of splendour in the grass' (line 181)? This kind of language provides a specially rapt and vibrant mode of argument, though the various items of the poem – lambs, shepherd boys, a single tree, a pansy at his feet, and so on – do not cohere, but this suits well the poem's assertion that the poet's perception of the world about him has lost its visionary intensity.

In Wordsworth's poetry by now we expect to find the objects of Nature animated, and this also is a common effect. This also often links an object with an idea or feeling:

> The moon doth with delight
> Look round her when the heavens are bare. (lines 12–13)

This is the only poem where Wordsworth puts forward the Platonic concept that our souls pre-exist our earthly existence: is this a figurative way of imagining the confidence of childhood, or does he mean the reader to take the idea literally? How are we to react to the assertion that a small child is 'best philosopher' (line 110) and 'Mighty Prophet! Seer blest!' (line 114)? Is this deliberate exaggeration to surprise us, standing our normal view on its head, like the paradox that the 'child is father of the man'? This section of the poem excited Coleridge's contempt in his *Biographia Literaria* (Chapter XXII), who grumpily asks 'in what sense is a child of that age a *philosopher*? In what sense does he *read* the eternal deep?' The 'Ode' is not a tentative exploration of a problem: it elaborates firm arguments, and therefore invites the reader's disbelief and disagreement.

Perhaps the best way of reading these passages is as strong illustrations of Wordsworth's anguish at growing old, and his fear of death: he envies what he perceives as the small child's uncaring, boundless confidence in its own immortality. Though the poem argues that there is strength and recompense in the 'years that bring the philosophic mind' (line 189), the over-riding impression that the poem leaves is one of dilution and loss. In terms of the imagery of light, which runs throughout the poem, though he is aware that 'the sun shines warm' (line 43) and he still enjoys 'the innocent brightness of a new-born day' (line 197), it is the sunset, 'the clouds that gather round the setting sun' (line 199), that the poet faces. It is the chill of old age and impending death that the poet feels even on the brightest spring day.

An ode is a specific form with a long history in English verse as well as in classical literature. A typifying feature is the serious subject matter and dignified form of the language. Another aspect of the form is the restless mixture of stanza and line lengths, and irregular rhymes, which are the perfect vehicle for Wordsworth's ranging, meditative, but magisterial argument.

Poems for comparison: 'To H.C., Six Years Old' (p. 283); Coleridge: 'Dejection: an Ode'

Paulò majora canamus let us now sing of greater things (from Virgil's *Eclogues* IV, i)

21   **tabor** a drum

'SURPRISED BY JOY, IMPATIENT AS THE WIND'   FROM *POEMS*, 1815 (p. 323)

Grief sharply revisited

In a moment of unexpected joy, the poet turns to share his pleasure with a loved one – only to remember that she is dead. It was love that brought this person to mind – but how could he have forgotten her? How could he have been beguiled into forgetting his loss, even for the tiniest amount of time? This moment of re-remembering was the worst pang of grief except for one other – that time he stood alone, knowing the person that he loved most was dead, and he would never see her face again.

The summary assumes that the poet is a man and the loved person is female, though the poem is not gender specific. In fact the poem refers to Wordsworth's grief for his daughter Catherine, who died aged three years and nine months in 1812.

This subtle and moving poem shows how the process of forgetting about grief becomes itself a cause of further grief, and of guilt. How could the poet be 'surprised by joy' (line 1) in a world bereft of his child? How could he have allowed himself to forget that she was no longer at his side? At the moment he turned to her, he relived his love, only to have it snatched away again.

We never learn what joy it was that distracted him, only that it makes him 'impatient as the wind' (line 1) to share it. Metaphorical language is minimal. Apart from this opening simile there is 'heart's best treasure' (line 12) and 'years unborn' (line 13); both of these add so little imaginative colour or specificity to the poem that they are almost dead metaphors. Nor is there any attempt to distract the reader from the poem's emotional argument with any sense of context or surroundings: only the poet's sudden movement – 'I wished to share the transport' (line 2) – offers a sense of a particular moment. On the other hand, the poem is subtly alliterative throughout, adding to its sense of cohesion and coherence.

The sonnet is perhaps unexpectedly a perfect form for this highly emotional and emotive poem. The succession of thoughts fits well with the general pattern of two quatrains and a sestet, with one interesting departure or irregularity: the second quatrain spills over into the sestet in a way that underlines the poet's shock that he has even for a moment forgotten about his loss. The enjambment between lines eight and nine is forced by an unexpectedly long sentence, leading to a heavy pause before the poem's resolution:

> Through what power...
> Have I been so beguiled as to be blind
> To my most grievous loss. That thought's return
> Was the worst pang ... (lines 6, 7–10)

The half-rhyme on 'return' (with 'forlorn' and 'unborn') also emphasises the terrible sense of loss at the poem's centre, in which grief springs ironically from joy.

Poem for comparison: 'A Slumber did My Spirit Seal' (p. 129)

2 **transport** having been carried away by emotion, as in 'transports of delight'
4 **vicissitude** change

THE PRELUDE: BOOKS I–II

NOTE ON THE TEXT

It is strange that Wordsworth should have decided that his long autobiographical poem was not to be published during his lifetime; instead he tinkered with it, altering and adjusting passages, though leaving the arrangement, content and sweep of the book intact. The result of this process of revision is that the poem now exists in several different texts. The form in which it was first read, reviewed and has most often been reprinted is the 1850 version, the final result of Wordsworth's emendations. There is a very early two-book version of 1799, which is sometimes printed in anthologies. In 1926 Ernest de Selincourt edited a text of 1805 using Wordsworth's manuscripts, the first full version of the 'Poem, Title not yet fixed upon … addressed to S.T. Coleridge'. Wordsworth read the poem to Coleridge, as well as addressing him throughout. Other friends also heard the poem in its early form; De Quincey published some of it from memory in his biographical writings on Wordsworth. *The Prelude* was the name Wordsworth's wife gave the poem when it was published a few months after his death in April 1850.

The 1850 text of *The Prelude* is in its language more concise and controlled. Wordsworth's changes seem to be aimed at making the diction of his autobiography more grandiose and impressive, eradicating what he might have come to feel was a too colloquial and confessional aspect. Certainly the earlier version leaves a more spontaneous, lively and personal impression; this is a document in the making, not one that has been worked over many times. The best way to judge this is to find one of the 'parallel' texts where the texts of 1850 and 1805 are printed alongside each other for the benefit of scholars and students of Wordsworth, and compare the wording of passages.

Because of its different, and in many respects more attractive language and overall impression, the 1805 version is now printed separately and commonly used as the authentic version of the text. It is this early version of the poem that these notes use, which will be found in *Wordsworth: The Prelude – The 1805 Text*, published by the Oxford University Press, 1970.

Note on the summaries

Detailed summaries of the Books I and II only are provided here; the remaining eleven books are summarised briefly. The two opening books lay the foundations for the account of the life that follows in *The Prelude*. In the justly celebrated passages describing his formative childhood, Wordsworth analyses the special relationship with his natural surroundings which is the premise of much of his poetry both before and after *The Prelude*.

Attempting to summarise a poem as long (8,477 lines) and as dense as *The Prelude* is fraught with difficulties. One problem is how to deal with a first-person narration. It seems peculiar to summarise in the first person, as if pretending to be Wordsworth – 'I did this, then I did that'. Yet what seems the more natural method, to re-work the narrative into the third person – discussing instead what 'Wordsworth' or 'the poet' did next – is to create an immediate falsification of tone and point of view, and to lose instantly one of the major effects of writing autobiographically – the sense of direct address to the reader. The third-person is used in the present summary, but readers should keep in mind the degree to which this translates the poetry into another form.

There is another problem special to this kind of autobiographical writing, to do with the tenses of the poem. Wordsworth often comments in the present tense on the life of ideas that he is reconstructing. He is writing from a present moment, or to be accurate, many moments, as the time of the poem's writing shifts throughout its length. But naturally he narrates the events his life in the past tense. The present tense is normally used for the purposes of commenting critically on texts, and for summarising. However, using the present tense to summarise *The Prelude* has the disadvantage of blurring Wordsworth's movement to and fro between the present commentary and narration of the past. For this reason the summaries employ the past tense for the poet's narration of past events,

y

and the present for his retrospective comments, though sometimes this may appear a bit stilted. (A further complication is that the first two verse paragraphs of the poem are in the present tense, to suggest an intense moment of creativity and composition.)

The numbers in brackets refer to the lines of the verse paragraphs summarised in the text that follows. An asterisk* draws attention to parts of the narrative where Wordsworth seeks to recreate in verse the experience of a specific 'moment' or scene.

BOOK FIRST: INTRODUCTION – CHILDHOOD AND SCHOOL-TIME

A moment of creativity – Wordsworth returns to the countryside – he longs to write but cannot find the right subject matter – his childhood, ruled by beauty and fear – poaching and boat-stealing episodes – skating – other childhood memories

The poet feels a 'gentle breeze' as he emerges from the prison of city-life. Where will he go? He is thrilled to feel that he is shaking off 'that burthen of my own unnatural self, / The heavy weight of many a weary day / Not mine.' (lines 1–32).

He is free to dedicate himself to his own activities, and feels within himself 'a corresponding mild creative breeze' which gives him hope that he can commit himself to poetry (lines 32–54).

Later he looks back at this moment of excitement described in the opening verse of the poem as a prophecy which gives him confidence (lines 55–67).

Then he describes how he lay on the ground on that beautiful autumn day, deciding where he would go, and imagining one particular 'sweet Vale' of his choice, till he was disturbed by the dropping of an acorn* (lines 68–94).

As evening approached, he set off on the journey towards his Vale. He tried again to compose poetry, but this time his creative powers were lacking. Shrugging off this disappointment, he decided to be content with present pleasures. Two days later he arrived at his destination (lines 95–115).

He found great happiness and love in the neighbourhood to which he had travelled, but very soon he wanted to dedicate himself to 'some determin'd aim'. He longed to pin down in visible form some of the ideas and feelings that had been 'floating loose' too long. But he could not do this; the sense of a creative dawn never turned into a full morning. His mind could not grapple with a 'noble theme' (lines 116–41).

He would like to have made progress with less weighty works, but poets are like lovers, subject to their 'unmanageable thoughts'. Even the meditative mind suffers from unquiet and distracting passions (lines 142–56).

When he looks into himself to see how suited he is to his 'glorious work', he is quite cheered. He has a 'vital soul', knowledge of 'general truths', forms and images, and a poet's skill. But he lacks a subject, or characters, perhaps some nearly forgotten names from history to whom he could give new life. At times he thinks he should tackle some British theme, perhaps a tale of chivalric knights, or an episode from the history of the Roman Empire, or the story of Liberty in Europe. Should he describe some unknown hero who suffered for truth, or concentrate on the battle against political oppression? Sometimes he decides to invent a story of his own, but this seems too insubstantial. His favourite aspiration is to compose a 'philosophic / Song of Truth' about ordinary life, but then he thinks this should wait till he is more mature. Thus he wastes time from day to day, finding many reasons for not being able to write anything, even 'simplicity and self-presented truth'. It would be better by far to 'stray about / Voluptuously through fields and rural walks' than endlessly be baffled by his own crushed ambitions and lack of accomplishment. Was it for this that the river Derwent 'flow'd along my dreams'? Its 'music' was the background to his childhood, giving him knowledge of the calm of Nature. This river was like a playmate. Often, as a small child, he delighted to bathe in it (lines 157–304).

His youth was a 'fair seed-time' for his soul, and he grew up 'Fostered alike by beauty and by fear'. He was lucky to have been born and to live where he did. As a nine-year-old he often used to hunt woodcocks in the mountains. He would go out alone at night, and sometimes steal birds snared by other hunters, leading to fearful guilty imaginings that he was being followed*. At other times, climbing dangerous crags to find ravens' eggs, he suddenly experienced a strange vision of the wind and sky* (lines 305–50).

The human mind is like harmony in music: 'there is a dark / Invisible workmanship that reconciles discordant elements'. Wordsworth is astonished that all the miseries, terrors, thoughts and feelings can coexist in his mind, when 'I am / Worthy of myself'. He believes that Nature will sometimes use 'severer interventions' in dealing with a favoured being (lines 351–71).

One evening he stole a boat and rowed out on to a lake in the moonlight*. Making stealthy progress towards the middle of the lake, he fixed his eye on a rocky crag above the cave from which he had stolen the boat. Suddenly a huge cliff became visible behind the crag, and as he rowed out, it seemed to be striding after him 'like a living thing'. Fearful, he turned round and took the boat back to the cave. After this his brain was filled with 'unknown modes of being': 'huge and mighty Forms' moved through his mind and troubled his dreams (lines 372–427).

Wordsworth expresses his thanks to 'the Spirit of the Universe' that from his earliest childhood his contact was with the 'enduring things' of nature, rather than the 'works of man', thus purifying his thoughts and feelings (lines 428–41).

This 'fellowship' with the things of nature was experienced at all times of day, and in all seasons; it was a kind of 'intercourse' (lines 442–51).

In winter, he enjoyed the rapture of skating with his friends well into the evening* (lines 452–73).

Sometimes he would skate off on his own, and suddenly stop, at which it seemed as if the cliffs still spun around him, as if he was feeling the earth rolling in its 'diurnal round' until everything went tranquil* (lines 474–89).

Wordsworth speculates that the 'ministry' of Nature must have had some purpose, associating all his passions and ideas with natural objects even during his 'boyish sports' (lines 490–501).

He decides to pursue this theme through the different seasonal activities (lines 501–504).

He describes gathering hazel nuts, fishing and kite-flying* (lines 505–24).

He remembers his love for the cottage where he lived. During winter the children played card games, while outside the rain fell, or they heard ice on the lake splitting* (lines 525–70).

As well as these violent 'extrinsic' passions, there were subtler experiences of Nature, pure moments of calm delight which from early childhood make us feel how we fit in the world (lines 571–84).

He remembers that even at the age of ten he 'held unconscious intercourse / With the eternal Beauty' of natural objects (lines 586–93).

He recalls the unreflective but extreme pleasure of watching the moon rising over the sea* (lines 594–608).

Often in the 'giddy bliss' of childhood pursuits he felt moments when the 'common face of Nature spake to me / Rememberable things'. Sometimes this was through chance coincidences, but even then such ideas might be food for mature thought later in life. The ever-present scenery remained in his mind. Thus by the alternation of fear and happiness the landscape became 'habitually dear' and 'Allied to the affections' (lines 609–40).

Wordsworth comments that he has begun his 'story' early, but is confident that Coleridge, the friend to whom the poem is addressed, will understand this. He hopes to 'fetch / Invigorating thoughts from former years' with which he can 'fix the wavering balance of my mind', and also now in his maturity spur himself on to 'honourable toil'. Even if he fails to understand or explain himself better, these 'recollected hours … have the charm / Of visionary things' and almost bring back the sensations of infancy (lines 640–63).

At least his mind has been 'revived' by what he has written, and so he decides to continue with 'the story of my life' (lines 664–71).

In spite of his lifelong interest in writing a 'philosophical poem' that would surpass all his other works, *The Prelude* remains Wordsworth's most significant long work. In its effort to explore the history of an individual consciousness it is the first major psychological auto-biography in English, and among the first of its kind in world literature. As mentioned in the 'Note on the Text' above, it was published after Wordsworth's death, though his revisions suggest that he maintained interest in the project. The poem's direct address to Coleridge – 'O Friend' (line 55); 'my Friend' (line 116); 'O dear Friend' (line 144) – and the comments that his fellow poet is a specially sympathetic and understanding listener, perhaps indicate how nervous Wordsworth is about embarking on a whole poem devoted to himself, initiated while he was still relatively young and unknown, and dedicated to describing the apparently inconsequential events and feelings of a life that had not yet arrived at distinction.

The poem is highly self-conscious, and is about self-consciousness; it circles about on itself, mulls and meditates, repeats, moves forward, and then repeats again. This is one of the many factors that make *The Prelude* a difficult text to read. As in 'Tintern Abbey' Wordsworth is attempting to enact the process of remembering, while trying also to express psychological and philosophical ideas about the nature of experience and memory. Perhaps anxiously, throughout the poem he keeps repeating in new formulations his central premises about childhood, the beneficent effects of contact with Nature, and the growth of his poetic sensibility. Another aspect of its difficulty is the high degree of abstraction in much of the writing, though not in the first two books, taken up as they are by highly concrete re-enactments of particular or generalised childhood experience. This is the main reason why for most readers the first two books remain their only contact with the poem.

The Prelude is a poem about the processes of writing. It begins in the present tense, with the poet feeling the thrill of a 'creative breeze' after, we understand, a period of misery and confinement, from which he is now freeing himself. Then he reflects upon this opening passage from some later moment (in Book VII we learn this is five years afterwards):

> Thus far, O Friend! did I, not used to make
> A present joy the matter of my Song,
> Pour out, that day, my soul in measur'd strains,
> Even in the very words which I have here
> Recorded. (lines 55–9)

His reflection on the passage leads into a description of how he decided to return to the countryside where he spent his childhood. This, in turn, leads into a lengthy account of the difficulties in settling upon a suitable subject matter for his poetic ambition, and in reaction to this – and in gratitude for the natural beauties that surround him – he slips into writing about his childhood. Feeling the rightness of this material, which inspires him to write well, he decides to continue remembering his boyhood pastimes in verse. And by the end of the first book he has determined upon an autobiographical project. He has slipped into finding what material suits him best. All the pompous subject matter is abandoned for the pleasure of remembering his childhood.

The Prelude is a prelude to a poetic career. The opening book of the poem deals with the search for appropriate subject matter, the states of mind in which creativity is blocked, the miseries of not being able to write, the fragility of the creative urge, subject as it is to the moods and miseries of the poet. The overall sweep of the poem offers a retrenchment in memory, the purpose of which is a re-dedication of poetic powers, and an understanding of the sources of a poetic sensibility, which in Wordsworth's psychology is closely allied to his mental stability. 'Imagination – How Impaired and Restored' is the title of Book XI of the poem. The disturbance out of which the poem grows is sometimes difficult to remember when reading the first two books, because on the one hand Wordsworth's poetry is so skilfully assured, and on the other he so often stresses, perhaps out of anxiety, his confidence in the restorative powers of and the blessings of Nature and the task of describing them.

The poem is itself a therapeutic exercise. Wordsworth hopes that his decision to describe his childhood will 'fix the wavering balance of my mind' (line 650). This is the purpose of the journey, the quest on which the poet embarks: by rediscovering, even re-enacting his life in the form of the poem, he hopes to trace the sources of his mental strength and weakness, in order to be able to move forwards. The poem grows out of dejection, despair, and a loss of confidence and belief in values. In our post-psychological world the idea that we can trace the origins of mental problems back to childhood experience, even in Wordsworth's phrase in 'Tintern Abbey', 'unremembered pleasures', is such a commonplace that it is difficult to recognise how innovative his project was in *The Prelude*. At this stage in the narrative, the poet does not know whether the project will be successful.

Readers are often puzzled by Wordsworth's emphasis on the role of fear as well as beauty in his moral education. In the episodes he chooses to relate, his childish terror is caused by the guilt involved in the thefts he describes, as is fully understood by the adult. The adult writer knows that the mountain *appears* to pursue him as a result of a common optical illusion, just as the giddiness caused by suddenly stopping skating makes the world *seem* to revolve around him. There is an interesting tension between the adult Wordsworth who writes and the boy who experiences the fear. These moments, when the ordinary habit-ruled perception of the world about him is fractured, provide a revelation of a new relationship with nature, but this is not primarily a mystical revelation, or if it has mystical aspects, it is not mysterious, but fully examined, analysed and explained by the adult writer. In the poetic enactment of the boat-stealing, opposites are balanced with fine craft – darkness and light, silence and sound, motion and stasis, surface and depth, lustful pleasure and guilty fear. The water over which he rows, with the stars above, is the essence of fluidity. The mountain, that should be fixed and permanent – more so even than the stars – suddenly changes its role, and becomes 'like a living thing' (line 411). A moment like this, so carefully and successfully re-created, acquires a pressure to mean much more than its originally trivial circumstance.

Wordsworth wants, in his examination of these episodes, to provide an intellectual elucidation of what he feels to be an absolute truth: that it was his relationship with his natural surroundings – woods, mountains, lakes – that led to his proper sense of morality and goodness. But he knows here that Nature's 'severer interventions' (line 370) are a matter of poetry, symbol and illusion, just as his personification of Nature – 'surely I was led by her' (line 372) – is a metaphorical mode of discussion, not a deification. The penetration of his youthful conscious mind by a new and disturbing sense of something ulterior and hidden – 'unknown modes of being' (line 420) – and the insight this provided into the fundamental make-up of mind and existence, goes far beyond any trite punishment meted out by Nature for stealing a boat.

It is the mind's capacity to cope with darkness and light, beauty and fear, the contrariety of human experience. Poetry, by bringing together and reconciling opposites, is mimicking an ordinary function of healthy mental activity:

> The Mind of Man is fram'd even like the breath
> And harmony of music. There is a dark
> Invisible workmanship that reconciles
> Discordant elements, and makes them move
> In one society. Ah me! that all the early miseries,
> Regrets, vexations, lassitudes, that all
> The thoughts and feelings which have been infuse'd
> Into my mind, should ever have made up
> The calm existence that is mine when I
> Am worthy of myself. (lines 351–61)

The self, 'soul' and 'mind' are sometimes interchangeable concepts for Wordsworth. Behind all the flux of experience and consciousness, the poem suggests, sometimes there is – or should be – a single, more coherent, calm, and unified 'self', one of greater 'worth' than all those chaotic, intervening, non-essential selves that should be ignored and discarded. The 'self' therefore has a moral aspect. Our minds or souls are naturally inclined towards betterment, Wordsworth suggests here, though as often in his poetry, his eloquence with regard to the 'miseries, / Regrets, vexations' suggests that the capacity to cope with things going wrong may be not entirely automatic and powerful .

The poem is imbued from its outset with a driving sense of the necessity to find the right path in a difficult, miserable world. Ironically, often in Wordsworth's poetry this can only be achieved by relaxing the adult intellect rather than adhering to the processes of reason. In this first book the poetic ambition is clear, but actual creativity results from a surrender to impulse and feeling. He slips into writing about childhood almost by sleight of hand – offering thanks to a river – and then he cheerfully observes at the end of the book that his composition seems to be moving ahead well enough, so he will continue in this vein.

104 **Aeolian visitations** an Aeolian harp was a stringed instrument in which the music was created by the wind; frequently used by the Romantics as a metaphor for poetry

186 **Mithridates** king of Pontus in Asia Minor, implacable opponent of the Roman Empire, who killed himself in 63BC

<dl>
<dd>188 Odin in Norse myth the supreme god</dd>
<dd>190 Sertorius Roman soldier who led a revolt in Spain against Sulla until he was assassinated in 72BC</dd>
<dd>205 that one Frenchman Dominique de Gourges, who in 1568 avenged a massacre of the French by the Spanish</dd>
<dd>211 Gustavus patriotic leader of the Swedes in their struggle against the Danes, later a successful king, died 1560</dd>
<dd>212 Dalecarlia's mines district of Sweden where Gustavus hid</dd>
<dd>214 Wallace Scottish patriot who fought the English, executed in 1305</dd>
<dd>234 Orphean lyre in Greek myth Orpheus was a poet and musician who unsuccessfully attempted to bring his wife Eurydice back from Hades; he was worshipped in a mystical cult</dd>
<dd>540 strife too humble to be named in verse noughts and crosses</dd>
</dl>

BOOK SECOND: SCHOOL-TIME – (CONTINUED)

**More childhood pastimes remembered – rowing and riding –
Nature sought for its own sake – impossibility of exactitude
in analysing habits of mind – examination of the
imagination of infants – rapt attention to landscape**

In lines 1–47 Wordsworth returns to describing the 'tumult' of his childhood games, prolonged for as long as possible on summer evenings*. He asks if there is anyone who would not give to 'duty and to truth' the eagerness of childish desire. His childhood seems so far away now that he seems to have 'Two consciousnesses, conscious of myself, / And of some other being'. When he returned to his village he found that a large rock which seemed to be central to his childhood has been split up to build an assembly room. He knows that many of his friends will remember the rock as it was, and the old lady who used to sell her wares nearby.

Gradually the 'boisterous race' of childhood matured into something calmer, though the beauties of Nature were still 'collaterally attached' to these calmer pastimes (lines 48–55).

In summer they went rowing on Lake Windermere, racing to different islands. Afterwards they would rest surrounded by the objects of nature which, Wordsworth believes, taught him independence and modesty, and 'the self-sufficing power of solitude' (lines 55–78).

Most of the time they were poor and ravenously hungry, but when they went back to school they could buy better food for picnics (lines 79–98).

Sometimes they could even afford to hire horses, riding them much further than they ought to have done, to visit a picturesquely ruined abbey, a haven of peace* (lines 99–121).

Then they would race off on their horses – leaving behind the statues and ivy-covered roofless walls. A wren once sang so beautifully there that he felt he could listen for ever*. Even when thunderously riding along the sandy beach, he would sometimes feel the presence of that 'still Spirit of the evening air' (lines 122–44).

There was a stylish modern inn on Windermere, built where there had once been a homely hut. There Wordsworth and his friend would play on the green. Sometimes, when they were returning home they would leave one of their number to play the flute as they rowed gently away*. Then the sky and the calm water would sink into his heart and hold him 'like a dream' (lines 145–80).

Thus were his 'sympathies enlarged'. He grew to love the sun, not in a rational way, but because it shone on the hills and mountains*. The moon also seemed to belong to his 'darling Vale' (lines 181–202).

The 'incidental charms' of Nature gradually grew weaker, and instead he started to seek it for its own sake. Who can spot the exact moment when a habit is sown like a seed, or point to exactly where each part of the 'river' of the mind was derived? Coleridge knows that science is not our glory, but a prop for human weakness. He knows that often the distinctions that we think we perceived are in fact our own inventions. He understands the 'unity of all'. It is indeed a hard task 'to analyse a soul' in which thoughts, habits and desires literally have no perceivable beginning (lines 203–37).

Wordsworth decides to trace 'the progress of our being'. He blesses the infant, who gathers 'passion from his mother's eye'. Feelings enter the baby like 'an awakening breeze'. An infant's mind is always eagerly trying to make sense of its surroundings. His mind 'spreads' tenaciously in the 'beloved presence' of the mother. By this everything around him is exalted. He is by no means an outcast: 'along his infant veins are interfus'd / The gravitation and the filial bond / Of nature, that connect him with the world'. Such a being occupies an 'active' world, in a constant and reciprocal relationship. His mind is part of one great mind, both creating and receiving. This active consciousness is 'the first / Poetic spirit of our human life'. In most people it is lost in adult life, but in some it is maintained (lines 237–80).

Wordsworth has tried to show how this 'infant sensibility' was sustained and strengthened by his childhood. A more difficult task lies ahead: he now has to describe how his mind became troubled. To start with he sought the visible world without knowing why. His mind grew open to subtler influences, especially small aspects of the objects already beloved to him. Every season brought with it a new and exciting knowledge of minute distinctions in his surroundings, whether he was in society or enjoying his solitude. He would listen in storm or calm to the sounds of nature, 'that are the ghostly language of the ancient earth, / Or make their dim abode in distant winds'. This gave him visionary power: remembering how he felt, not what he felt, gives him a sense of 'possible sublimity', to which his soul can aspire (lines 280–341).

The 'universal power' in the 'essences of things', the source of delight, becomes strengthened and 'superadded'. Wordsworth describes how he liked to walk in the early morning, often with a friend. Sometimes he would sit contemplating the countryside in front of him, and be overcome by a 'holy calm', till he forgets that he has 'bodily eyes', and sees the view 'like something in myself, a dream, / A prospect in my mind' (lines 341–71).

It would take too long to describe all the circumstances by which he retained 'that spirit of religious love in which / I walked with Nature', and kept his 'first creative sensibility'. He had within him a 'plastic power', sometimes rebellious, which made him at odds with 'general tendency' but which was in tune with his surroundings. It heightened the beauty of the sun, the birds, the winds, water and storms (lines 371–95).

He also wants to explain an activity which he regards more highly than analytic thought: the creative observation of secret affinities between things. He used to invest objects with feelings and see 'blessings spread around me like a sea'. With 'bliss ineffable' he felt 'the sentiment of Being spread / O'er all that moves'. In all Nature and its movements he sensed one joyful life, one song, inaudible to the 'fleshly ear' (lines 395–434).

Even if these beliefs are wrong, Wordsworth wishes to express his gratitude to the mountains, lakes, waterfalls and weathers in which he spent his childhood. Their gift has been his purity of heart, and the capacity to commune with God and Nature. Even in a time like the present when good men are given up to apathy or wickedness, a time of 'dereliction and dismay', he does not despair. His confidence and faith are the gift of Nature, which has fed his 'lofty speculations', and provided 'a never-failing principle of joy, / And purest passion' (lines 435–66).

Coleridge, his addressee, started life differently, but has arrived at the same worship of Nature (lines 466–79).

He finishes by wishing Coleridge good health and a long life (lines 479–84).

In the passage of commentary with which this book starts, Wordsworth puts into his own language the friction between memory of the child's experience and the adult's retrospective understanding which is a commonplace of autobiographical writing:

> ... so wide appears
> The vacancy between me and those days,
> Which yet have such self-presence in my mind
> That, sometimes, when I think of it, I seem
> Two consciousnesses, conscious of myself
> And of some other Being. (lines 28–33)

'Self-presence' is a typical proto-psychological compound word, created in the effort to pin down his perceptions about the functioning of his mind. These 'two consciousnesses' are mirrored in the narrative method of the poem, in the interchange between the past tense, in which memories are recalled, and the present tense of interpretation. This is the characteristic pattern of *The Prelude*, in which the narration of a memory is followed by reflection and explanation. Book II has no such outstanding stretch of highly wrought poetry as the boat-stealing episode of the first book. There are memorable accounts of communal and repeated activities, but they are more generalised, and the resulting poetic descriptions do not arrive at the same state of autonomy.

The impossibility of exactly pin-pointing the origins of habits of mind leads Wordsworth into a consideration of the 'infant sensibility' which is the 'Great birthright of our Being' (lines 285–6).

This is a key passage for understanding his view of the imagination. Babies occupy an 'apprehensive habitude' (line 256), a space where others are constantly acting on their behalf. They are constantly in the care of others. Their world is, indeed, an '*active*' (line 257) portion of the universe, but they still need to exercise their imagination to understand the world about them. They are:

> … eager to combine
> In one appearance, all the elements
> And parts of the same object, else detach'd
> And loth to coalesce. (lines 246–50)

In order to perceive anything, Wordsworth argues, an active imaginative act takes place whereby the multiplicity of an object is understood as unified. Without eagerly exercising this primary creative understanding, the child would exist in a world of bits and pieces where nothing related to anything else. Everyone as an infant possesses this power, though in most of us it is diminished or lost:

> Such, verily, is the first
> Poetic spirit of our human life;
> By uniform control of after years
> In most abated or suppress'd, in some …
> Pre-eminent till death. (lines 275–80)

The poetic imagination is simply a continuation of the basic activity of perception, in those, like Wordsworth, who are favoured beings. He is ever mindful of the luck involved in his upbringing that resulted in the preservation and augmentation of this poetic power. *The Prelude* seeks to examine and define the circumstances of by which this 'poetic spirit' – the 'Great Birthright of our Being' can be 'augmented and sustained' (lines 286–8). When a baby exercises its powers of perception in response to feelings which are gathered from a 'Mother's eye', it feels an 'awakening breeze' (line 245). This is the same as the 'creative breeze' with which the poem began, the wind of poetic creation which is one of the major symbols of **Romantic** poetry.

---

219 **succedaneum** a substitute

THE PRELUDE: BOOKS III—XIII: SHORT SUMMARIES

BOOK THIRD: RESIDENCE IN CAMBRIDGE

The motley spectacle of Cambridge – relationship with Nature deepens – the genius of humanity – his studies – pros and cons of University life

Wordsworth describes his wonder at arriving in Cambridge, and finding himself, 'a mountain youth', moving in society of a kind new to him. His rooms were an 'obscure nook' in St John's College. He did not really fit into this different world, and often found himself seeking solitude in the flat Cambridge countryside. He remembers how there he also endowed every detail of nature with a moral life, which leads him to wonder at the 'divinity' and 'power' of the human mind, and its creative capacity. All men, he argues, must have their god-like moments, realising their power 'as natural beings in the strength of nature' (line 194).

Wordsworth admits that, though he enjoyed solitude, he was naturally gregarious, and drawn to 'idleness and joy' (line 236). His 'Imagination slept' (line 260). The famous writers who had been at Cambridge held some sway over him. One night in a room supposedly once occupied by Milton, he made himself drunk by drinking toasts to that great poet. He became vain. Wordsworth criticises his past self for fecklessness, and his incapacity to take his studies seriously, but the spirit of academic life – and even that of the Church – seemed to be 'Folly and False-seeming' (line 410). The life of the scholar must have been more rigorous in the olden days. Yet he has no regrets; he fell into a shallow rather than a wicked way of life. His 'under soul', meanwhile was 'hushed' and 'lock'd up' (line 540). He had no taste for the artificiality of society, and expresses dislike for the old dons, who compare very unfavourably with the old men he knew back at home. Cambridge was no more than 'a creek of the vast sea' (line 626) in relation to his real life. His student days were like wandering around a museum, marvelling at bits and pieces, but only remembering a little; nine months there were spent in 'submissive idleness' (line 669).

The description of Cambridge in this Book illustrates a kind of poetic writing unlike that which the reader has encountered so far in

The Prelude. We are aware from the opening of the poem that Wordsworth is escaping from the city to the countryside. Here, for the first time, he describes a busy city with its sophisticated social and literary life. His language becomes more clipped and precise, even witty, as in his description of Newton's statue, with its slightly contorted syntax and odd conjunction of face and a scientific instrument, redolent of eighteenth-century poetry:

> The Antechapel, where the statue stood
> Of Newton, with his prism and silent Face. (lines 58–9)

The main focus of the Book, however, is the moral education that Cambridge failed to provide, but which is forged in his continuing visionary perception of the natural world about him. Wordsworth continues the careful definition of this special relationship in language that recalls the activity of infant perception in Book II. He looks at the world about him for 'universal things' and:

> ... perused
> The common countenance of earth and heaven
> And, turning the mind in upon itself,
> Pored, watch'd, expected, listen'd; spread my thoughts
> And spread them with a wider creeping. (lines 110–14)

He personifies Nature – whose 'chosen son' (line 82) he is; but at the same time watches the reciprocal development of the relationship in his own mind. His strengthening Pantheism (see Part Three, Nature and Pantheism) in *The Prelude* is explained in terms of rational psychological analysis. Passages like this show how his trust in Nature's powers is far from being a primitive, simple or naïve faith; rather his beliefs have to be worked out in the poetry. Throughout the poem Wordsworth is in the process of constantly re-evaluating this complex relationship between the individual mind, which perceives the outside world, and the imagination which first makes sense of this experience, and then recreates that experience in the form of poetry.

It is sometimes impossible for the viewer to separate the viewing self from what it views: 'I was the Dreamer, they the Dream' (line 27) he remarks of Cambridge, just as in Book II his favourite valley becomes 'like something in myself, a dream, / A prospect in my mind' (line 370–1). Dreams for Wordsworth represent a heightened perception of reality, not something vague and mysterious. Poetry, as heightened language, is the appropriate vehicle for this vision.

Book III contains a description of Wordsworth's 'genius' which is a key piece in the jigsaw of his argument about the imagination and his choice of the autobiographical mode of writing:

> ... Of Genius, Power,
> Creation, and Divinity itself
> I have been speaking, for my theme has been
> What passed within me. (lines 171–4)

He has not been describing 'outward things' but of his 'own heart' (line 176). He wonders at 'the might of Souls / And what they do within themselves' (lines 178–9). The world is nothing but a 'wild field' (line 181) where they were sown. This is 'heroic argument' (line 182), the proper material for writing, though ultimately it may be inexpressible:

> It lies far hidden from the reach of words.
> Points have we all of us within our souls
> Where all stand single; this I feel, and make
> Breathings for incommunicable powers.
> Yet each man is a memory to himself... (lines 185–9)

For Wordsworth, 'genius' is something that we all possess.

Organic metaphors, such as the idea that souls are seeds sown in a 'wild field' permeate *The Prelude*. The river is a comparable image for the meandering and accumulative growth of mind and personality – the 'river' of his mind in Book I, line 214, for example. A yet more pervasive strand of thematic imagery, well illustrated in Book III, is the journey. The poet journeys through life – and in Wordsworth's case experience very often consists literally of a journey, given his love for walking tours – and the poem consists of a journey into the past, and into the nature of memory and mind. The narrative ascends to heights:

> 'and here ... have I retrac'd my life
> Up to an eminence ... (lines 178–9).

And tackles less exalted subjects:

> Enough: for now into a populous Plain
> We must descend – A Traveller I am,
> And all my tale is of myself. (lines 195–6)

Every twist of behaviour and thought may be accommodated into the metaphor. When Wordsworth repeats his habit of giving moral life to natural forms, he remarks that he is pursuing 'A track …not untrod before' (lines 121). This imagery of a journey through countryside – tracks, mountains, plains – is knit into the different narrative strands so as to be almost unnoticeable, yet it serves subtly to underline the unity of Wordsworth's way of thinking and writing, making the landscape – that landscape he loves and regards as so significant in his personal development – into a map for his mind, for his past life, and for the intellectual journey that the poem pursues. The literal and the figurative interconnect, just as Wordsworth himself interconnects with the landscape, often so he cannot tell whether it is in his mind or outside him.

BOOK FOURTH: SUMMER VACATION

Return to the Lake District – the pleasures of being at home again – transcendental experience of nature – yet Wordsworth is often distracted – further dedication to poetry – midnight encounter with a vagrant soldier

In summer Wordsworth returned to 'that sweet Valley where I had been rear'd' (line 11). In memory he blesses the Dame who looked after him. She was delighted to see him. At rediscovering familiar things like his bed and his dog, he felt intense pleasure, mixed with memories of the experiences attached to them. On one of his old walks he felt especially reinvigorated, sitting under a hazel tree*, it was as if his soul 'had put off her veil' and 'stood / Naked in the presence of her God' (lines 141–2). He saw the familiar village folk with a new affectionate irony. His delight in Nature and the stars had deepened. In a sustained description of a man in a boat, looking into water, and not being able to distinguish clearly between what is reflected in the water and what is under the water*, Wordsworth finds the image for the process of re-examining the past in which he is involved. But he has to admit that in spite of new pleasures, there was an 'inner falling off' (line 270): he seemed sometimes to be surrounded by 'contagious air' (line 290).

Returning at dawn from a party, however, he had a full experience of the beauties of Nature* that made him a 'dedicated spirit' (line 344). His mind was muddled; it was a 'strange rendezvous' for the 'grave and gay' (line 346). In a long passage he describes his habit of walking the roads at night, and a specific encounter with a scrawny tramp. This old man was propped against a milestone muttering to himself. Wordsworth watched him for some time, then engaged him in conversation, and after hearing about his destitute state, took him to a peasant's cottage where he knew he would be given food and lodging.

> The triple narrative of Wordsworth's relationships with nature, with humanity, and with his vocation as a poet is continued and developed in Book IV by a series of incidents and insights. On an evening walk he experiences 'consummate happiness' (line 130) and a sense of tranquil restoration which is indeed mystical in its intensity:

> > Gently did my soul
> > Put off her veil, and, self-transmuted, stood
> > Naked as in the presence of her God. (lines 140–2)

> Is his image for the soul a nun, who is a bride of Christ, or something more pagan? Such language of worship, erotic in its intensity, is not untypical of Christian mystical writing, but it is a new stage in Wordsworth's narrative of his rapport with his surroundings. He has explained how 'cold and raw' (line 135) the evening is, and this, by contrast, makes the metaphor of nakedness even more striking.

> Another interesting use of figurative language is the extended simile which Wordsworth develops, of a man looking into still water from a boat. He sees below him all the underwater life of weeds and fish as well as stones and pebbles, yet his vision is confused by reflections in the water:

> [he] is perplex'd, and cannot part
> The shadow from the substance, rocks and sky,
> Mountains and clouds from ... the things which there abide
> In their true dwelling. (lines 255–8)

The reader wonders to what this simile, developed over thirteen lines, will apply. It transpires that it describes the process in which the narrative is involved, 'incumbent o'er the surface of past time' (line 263), pleasurably sifting through memories which are tangled and intermixed with each other and with present experience of the past written as poetry. Wordsworth shows here his realisation that the practice of autobiographical writing is not simply a matter of recounting a collection of facts, but a creative process of choice and selection.

Book IV finishes with a long account of his night-time meeting with a mumbling tramp, a retired soldier trying to make his way home. Wordsworth's habit of enjoying lonely walks on public roads in the dark is something of a calculated oddity, as is his particular interest in vagrants. Wordsworth is surprised out of contented meditation by the unexpected sight of another, and he starts by hiding in fear of this 'uncouth shape' (line 402), and then observes him intently. The sudden switch from deep private thought to intense awareness of something outside himself is a common pattern in his poetry, and displays his curiosity about habits of consciousness. His particular interest in beggars, vagrants and others stranded at the margins of society is discussed below in relation to 'Resolution and Independence' (pp. 38–42)

BOOK FIFTH: BOOKS

Human achievements, unlike Nature, are not immortal – a strange dream about books – Wordsworth's views on education – the boy who hooted at the owls – incident of a drowned man – Wordsworth's childhood reading and its effects

Thinking about human intellectual endeavour makes Wordsworth sad. Man has created things which, unlike 'the speaking face of earth and heaven' (line 11) will not achieve immortality. Even if earthquake and fire were to dry up the sea, the 'living Presence' (line 33) would still 'subsist', but the works of man will not endure.

He once confided this view to a friend, who admitted having the same thought. This friend fell asleep while reading Cervantes by the sea, and dreamed that in a desert he met an Arab on a dromedary who was carrying a stone and a shell, which the Arab asserts are books. The stone is the book of geometry, the Arab explains, but the shell is more valuable. Listening to the shell, the dreamer hears a poem foretelling the destruction of humankind. The Arab's mission is to bury his 'books', and, turning half into Don Quixote, he rushes off to avoid drowning in a sudden flood, which wakes the dreamer in terror.

Wordsworth is struck by this dream. When he holds a great book of poetry in his hand, he shares something of the Arab's anxiety. He looks back on what he has written of his childhood so far, and wonders what was the point of writing about such familiar material. He realises that all literature, from the epic to the ballad, has its value, though always less than 'Nature's self which is the breath of God' (line 222).

The poet expresses his gratitude that his childhood was spent in relative freedom, not cursed by an overpowering educative system. His mother, who died when he was young, wisely did not try to force her children, but left them space to develop naturally. Wordsworth fears that pushing children too hard can turn them into 'dwarf' men (line 295), overstuffed with adult skills and knowledge, and knowing nothing of the simple beauties of Nature. Such an education is a hollow lie, based on vanity. Children should enjoy childish things, such as fairy tales. Modern educators turn children into unnatural machines.

He tells the story of the boy who blew 'mimic hootings to the silent owls / That they might answer him' (lines 398–9; see 'There was a boy', pp. 126, Selected Poems). He blesses the village school, where children grow up free to play and learn, a 'race of real children, not too wise, / Too learned or too good' (lines 436–7).

When at the age of nine he saw a drowned man taken from the lake, Wordsworth had no fear, because the ghastly sight was perceived through his reading of fairy stories, which turned it into poetry. His childhood ambition to own all four volumes of the much-loved 'Arabian Tales' was never fulfilled. He was a voracious reader. Children are naturally drawn to imaginative stories of marvels and derring-do, that feed their 'hidden appetites' (line 530). He blesses the dreamers who write this kind of powerful literature, though it is condemned by 'the ape / Philosophy' (lines 549–50). Eventually children begin to enjoy 'sober truth' (line 566), but Wordsworth is sad that the rapturous reading of childhood passes away. By the age of thirteen he was drawn to the sound of language for its own sake. As he walked through the countryside with friends, they would recite verse, thrilled by 'airy fancies / More bright than madness or the dreams of wine' (lines 591–2). Wordsworth tries to unravel the special relationship that he believes exists between the enjoyment of Nature and poetry.

> The title of this book is odd in relation to its contents: there is very little discussion of books, except to start with as one of the products of transient human culture, and later as playing a general part in the imaginative education of children. At its centre is a strange dream – not even Wordsworth's own dream, he says, but that of a friend who shares his view of the volatility of civilisation – about an Arab on a dromedary, attempting to save two symbolic books from the end of the world by flood. On the one hand this chapter is an almost entirely abstract debate about education (only the depiction of the boy Wordsworth's witnessing the emergence of a corpse from a lake arrives at any kind of detailed concrete description).

> What is the meaning of the dream? Of course, the choice to use a dream in this way means that a search for a clear 'meaning' is likely to prove elusive. Wordsworth must want it to remain something of an enigma, so that we puzzle over its possibilities, otherwise why use this tangential, symbolic mode of argument?

> The dream has a special place in the thinking of the **Romantic** poets, including Wordsworth, though he most often uses it as a metaphor to describe heightened moments of daytime experience. For thinkers intent on valuing rationality above all else, the dream is likely to be simply perceived as a meaningless contrariety, the source of falsehood, delusion, even wickedness. The Spanish artist Goya in his etching entitled 'The Sleep of Reason Produces Monsters' (in *Caprichos*, 1799) depicts a writer asleep at his desk, while around him flit nightmarish owls and bats. Wordsworth shows here that instead

he sees it as a mode of knowledge, a way of approaching even the most serious of subjects.

Wordsworth's friend fell asleep while reading Cervantes, and the Arab turns into Don Quixote at the end of the dream. The figure of Don Quixote is essentially connected to the nature of books. The eccentric knight is driven crazy by reading too many mediaeval romances filled with stories of ogres and abandoned maidens, so that he takes up arms and sets out on his own quest in a world where there are no such imaginary inhabitants or situations. Seeing only with the distorted vision of the romance-reader, he attacks windmills which he believes are giants. Is Wordsworth saying that any attempt to preserve the objects of human culture is ultimately bound to be a Quixotic failure? Are literature and even mathematics as insubstantial and misleading as the books that drove Don Quixote mad? These are some of the issues and ideas that the dream raises.

Later Wordsworth praises the *Arabian Nights* (called by him 'Arabian Tales'), exotic and imaginary stories, as his favourite childhood reading. He argues that fairy tales are the proper kinds of book for children. In this he is taking up a position against those educationalists who prefer more realistic, moral and overtly serious reading material. As a peculiar demonstration of the way in which his imagination was enriched, he maintains that the horrific experience of seeing a drowned man dredged from the lake was idealised in his childish mind; his way of interpreting the event as if in the visionary world of fairy-tale, insulates him from the real horrors of the experience.

These arguments about the relationship between the imaginary worlds of literature and day-to-day reality are at the centre of **Romantic** thinking, though obsessive worrying at this divergence was to be at the heart of Keats's poetry, not Wordsworth's. Here Wordsworth argues that the power of imaginative thinking fostered by reading non-realistic books provides an indispensable filter for children dealing with the grim world of adult reality. The dream of the Arab suggests implicitly that it is human to wish to preserve human civilisation in the adversity of the desert and the flood. On the other hand he is only too conscious of the short-lived fragility of cultural artefacts. Indeed he seems confidently pessimistic about the future of human civilisation, which, unlike the world of Nature (which encompasses earthquake and flood), will not endure.

BOOK SIXTH: CAMBRIDGE AND THE ALPS

Cambridge again – poetic ambitions and study interests – holiday in the Dales – Coleridge's different life – a walking tour through France to Switzerland and Italy – crossing the Alps

Back at Cambridge, he found himself less attracted to the social whirl, and studied quite hard – though not according to any plan. He lacked the confidence to follow his own instincts, though he was full of poetic ambition. A particular tree captured his imagination*. Geometry fascinated him, as an image of God. He was also drawn to melancholy.

In the summer he went walking with his sister and another 'Maid' (line 233). Wordsworth looks back with such pleasure at this season that he imagines that Coleridge was there with them. He wonders at how close he and Coleridge are, in spite of their different backgrounds. He imagines the other poet's life at school, and wishes they had met earlier.

After three years as a student, he set off for a walking tour of the Alps with a fellow mountaineer. France was in the grip of political excitement, and they were open-heartedly entertained by joyful crowds. They walked around Switzerland with 'military speed' (line 478). Mont Blanc was disappointing, but the Vale of Chamonix was impressive*. On the Simplon Pass they lost their way, and were disillusioned to find that they had crossed the Alps without really noticing. This setback was rectified by a strikingly gloomy chasm that seemed like an image of 'the types and symbols of Eternity'* (line 571). The sunshine of Italy was delightful, in spite of a night spent lost on the shores of Lake Como, being bitten by insects.

Wordsworth explains that his experience of the magnificence of the Alps added to, and did not eclipse, earlier experiences of the natural world. They left a Europe on the thrilling verge of the struggle for Liberty.

Perhaps Wordsworth's poetry works best when his language seems charged with the particularity of a specific remembered incident, as is the case with many of his childhood memories in the early books of

The Prelude. In the final books Wordsworth dwells on the special meaning these specific memories ('spots of time') have for him (see pp. 95–7). Here in this middle part of the poem there are also occasional such 'spots of time' that seem separable from the narrative, almost like short autonomous poems in their own right (indeed 'There was a boy' in Book V was published separately as a short poem). One such is the account of a chasm in which Wordsworth finds himself after crossing the Simplon Pass between Switzerland and Italy.

Wordsworth is curiously disappointed by the Alps. It is an abyss that captures his imagination, not a mountain. Mont Blanc, the highest mountain in Europe, and one that features largely in other writers' accounts of their journeys through Switzerland, is dismissed by Wordsworth in a few lines:

> That day we first
> Beheld the summit of Mont Blanc, and griev'd
> To have a soulless image on the eye
> Which had usurp'd upon a living thought
> That never more could be. (lines 452–6)

The sight of the mountain – now just a visual image – does not live up to the 'living thought' of his expectation and hopes; his idea of Mont Blanc has been usurped by reality. This is a hazard of the imagination: rather than enhancing or transforming 'real' experience, instead it may lead to disappointment and diminishment.

Almost comically, Wordsworth finds by mistake that he has crossed the Alps, and narrowly missed noticing and recording the event. It is not the thrilling moment that it should have been. Imagination 'came athwart me; I was lost as in a cloud' (line 529). But he argues that imagination is still a beneficent force, even in 'such strength / Of usurpation' (lines 532–3). It is human nature to dwell with infinitude:

> With hope it is, hope that can never die,
> Effort, and expectation, and desire,
> And something evermore about to be. (lines 540–2)

The 'spoils or trophies' (line 544) – crossing the Alps or seeing Mont Blanc – are as nothing to the 'access of joy' (line 547) of the hopeful imagination. And as a demonstration of this, the impressive descent into the 'narrow chasm' (line 523) immediately follows, and provides a focus for Wordsworth's poetic and imaginative powers.

It is typical of *The Prelude* to move so swiftly from such a passage of manifest seriousness – portentousness, even – in which the culmination of a description of landscape is that it resembles the 'Characters of the great Apocalypse' (line 570) to a mundane comment on the unnecessary largeness of the 'high and spacious rooms' in an Alpine hostel. As so often, Wordsworth's autobiography provides a 'confluence of two Streams' (line 576) indeed, this text is often the focus for many more than two 'streams' of thought. Like all attempts to describe the contents of consciousness, it is a meeting point for innumerable different discourses. Here we see the practical guidebook to Switzerland following on from a bravura demonstration in reading and writing landscape, and being succeeded itself by a highly figurative comment on the quality of a night's sleep. 'Innocent Sleep' alludes to Shakespeare's *Macbeth* (II.2.36), though the personification is here extended, so that it is made to 'lie melancholy among weary bones' (line 580) almost as if it is a graveyard.

Wordsworth has just crossed the Alps, after having lost his way: this is the message in 'the tidings' (line 550) given him by a peasant. In his travels he has been disappointed with Mont Blanc, but now he finds himself going downhill into a 'chasm' (line 553), something like the opposite of a mountain, but equally redolent of poetic symbolism, so far as Wordsworth and his fellow poets were concerned, for the way it contains energies and oppositions. In his poem 'This Lime-Tree Bower My Prison' (1800) Coleridge describes a 'dell', less impressive than a chasm, but which has many interesting parallels with the passage above, but his most famous example is undoubtedly in 'Kubla Khan' (written 1797–8, published 1816):

> But Oh! that deep romantic chasm which slanted
> Down the green hill athwart a cedarn cover!
> A savage place! as holy and enchanted
> As e'er beneath a waning moon was haunted
> By woman wailing for her demon lover!

From this chasm, 'a mighty fountain momently was forced' which flung up 'the sacred river', a collection of images which is usually taken to refer to the activity of the imagination.

Wordsworth starts by describing the way the brook and the road 'were fellow-travellers' (line 554), both with each other and with the two walkers. To begin with they 'hurried fast' (line 552) but now they progress at 'a slow step' (line 556) for several hours. What follows is a collection of images of the chasm, nearly every one of which contains or suggests oppositions between ideas. Language is the only medium in which such an account could be created. These oppositions are easiest to display in list form, spelling out the logical incongruities that metaphor allows:

- if something has 'height', can it be 'immeasurable'?
- the woods are 'decaying' but 'never to be decay'd'
- 'blasts of waterfalls' cannot be 'stationary'
- the 'rent' cannot be 'hollow' as we know what it contains
- the winds are thwarting each other, but also 'bewilder'd and forlorn'
- torrents cannot 'shoot from the clear blue sky'
- rocks cannot mutter
- crags cannot 'drizzle' or speak
- the stream cannot rave
- clouds cannot be either fettered or 'unfetter'd'.

At the 'sick sight / And giddy prospect' (line 564–5) the poet seems nauseated by the contrast between looking down at the stream, and up at the sky above. The chasm or 'rent' contains the elemental water, rocks and airy sky, described in terms of impossible oppositions fashioned by dense metaphorical description. To sum up, Wordsworth specifies the chief oppositions in terms of abstractions: 'Tumult and peace, the darkness and the light' (line 567). But then he brings them together into a series of images of coherence and unity: they are 'like workings of one mind, the features / Of the same face, blossoms upon one tree' (lines 568–9). And these unified oppositions are:

y

> Characters of the great Apocalypse,
> The types and symbols of Eternity,
> Of first, and last, and midst, and without end. (lines 570–3)

'Characters' (letters) is an image from written language (as are 'types and symbols'). Meaning inscribed or written in Nature has to be read, and what the chasm stands for is the Apocalypse, the revelation of the end of the world, when time also will end. But it is also the type and 'symbol of Eternity', timelessness, the 'first, and last, and midst, and without end', the concluding line of many Christian prayers, invoking the everlasting presence of God.

Perceiving and capturing oppositions in the description of the chasm might be sufficient in itself, but Wordsworth's assertion that these contradictions 'were all like workings of one mind, the features / Of the same face, blossoms upon one tree' (lines 568–9) takes the intrinsic poetic argument in a different and perhaps unexpected direction. It is a motivating belief expressed in *The Prelude* that it is the natural function of the mind to harmonise contradictory aspects of experience:

> The mind of man is fram'd even like the breath
> And harmony of music. There is a dark
> Invisible workmanship that reconciles
> Discordant elements and makes them move
> In one society. (Book I, lines 351–5)

As he demonstrates on so many occasions it is the imagination, the active process of perceiving and thereby making relationships between things, that works to achieve this unity.

The chasm passage is one of the many 'moments' that intersperse and vivify *The Prelude* (see the discussion of 'spots of time' on pp. 95–7). Throughout the poem Wordsworth is aware that he is writing experimentally, and often draws attention to his new techniques or discoveries.

'Symbol' is now commonplace word as a literary term, but at the time Wordsworth was writing this use was unusual if not unique. It would have ceased to be unusual by the time *The Prelude* was published after his death in 1850; *Les Fleurs du Mal* by Baudelaire, a **symbolist** poet, was published only seven years later.

Words, whether spoken or written, are already themselves symbols, signs in sound or squiggles on paper for something other than themselves. The poet is already dealing in symbols when writing. Wordsworth's chasm exists in words that are carefully chosen so as to invent a verbal structure that does not represent a 'real' chasm, since it is full of logical impossibilities. It, too, is a symbol, for the abstractions – Apocalypse and Eternity – that the poet reads or writes into the landscape he describes by his creative act. As Wordsworth expresses it in 'Tintern Abbey' (see pp. 24–30), this is:

> ... the mighty world
> Of eye and ear, both what they half-create,
> And what perceive.

Book SEVENTH: RESIDENCE IN LONDON

The 'creative breeze' remembered – London – its sights – the 'Maid of Buttermere' – places visited – Bartholomew Fair – reflection on the city and Nature

Wordsworth looks back to the moment of the 'creative breeze' (at the start of *The Prelude*) five years from his present time of writing. He only started writing last spring, but has stopped during the summer, and now the song of robins, and a last lonely glow-worm remind him that winter is approaching, and this fills him full of 'chearful hope' (line 54).

After university he went to London, a city of which he knew nearly nothing except its fabled reputation; he was full of 'fond imaginations' (line 136), but the reality, though somewhat disappointing, still filled him with keen pleasure. There follows a lengthy panorama of the 'motley imagery' (line 150) of London life*, the streets crowded with carriages and every imaginable kind of person. Out of the various different kinds of show on offer, what interested him particularly was 'The Maid of Buttermere', a drama about a young woman whom he knew in the Lake District. Remembering her dead illegitimate baby reminds him of an innocent 'rosy Babe' he saw, his mother with a painted face, surrounded by 'dissolute men / And shameless women' (lines 387–8).

He loved the theatre; plays affected him strongly, but only in 'the suburbs of the mind' (line 507). He also visited the Law Courts, the House of Lords, and churches.

One lasting impression was the oppressive throngs of unknown faces. A blind beggar sticks in his memory. He describes Bartholomew Fair, with its stalls and freak shows, a scene of 'blank confusion' (line 696), that serves as an image for the whole city. Wordsworth feels that through his consciousness of the enduring natural world, 'the mountain outline, and its steady forms' (line 723), he managed even in London to sense 'the Soul of Beauty' and harmony behind 'the press / Of self destroying, transitory things' (lines 739–40).

It comes as something of a surprise to locate the opening of the poem, when Wordsworth poured forth his excitement at returning to his beloved countryside, as five years previous to the moment of writing Book VII. The reader has followed the narrative of childhood, boyhood, student days, a walking tour – London seems a natural next stage in the recounting of his life. Yet Wordsworth wants to remind us of real time passing during the writing of the poem – perhaps a puzzlingly lengthy interval – as well as the steady narrative time of his development. This revelation pushes the memory of London further into the past, and raises the question as to what Wordsworth has been doing in the interim.

Throughout this account of his stay in London, Wordsworth seems no more than a spectator, looking on at what he sees, with no sense of participation or belonging. The mystery of how he supported himself during this time is cleared up in Book XIII – but clearly he has no need to think of London as a place of work or endeavour. He is interested to see a story of the Lake District – the 'Maid of Buttermere' – literally on show as an exotic tale of vice and virtue; he seems drawn towards and comforted by anything that is remotely familiar. Throngs of faces, innocent children surrounded by vicious adults, beggars, loose women – this is the London as depicted in the painter Hogarth's moralising paintings and engravings, such as 'The Rake's Progress' (c. 1735). The place that Wordsworth chooses as an emblem of the city's confusion and dissipation is Bartholomew Fair, exactly as it had been used by seventeenth-century playwrights as a focus of London's excesses; Ben Jonson's rambunctious play of the same name, an attack on Puritans, was performed in 1614. Wordsworth seems only shocked and horrified by the busy activity of the performers and the crowds. The people 'swarm' (line 699) or are described as 'vomiting' from the tents and booths (line 694). He takes a moral view of the 'low pursuits' (line 701). Wordsworth shows himself incapable of imagining that anything good can grow out of this 'blank confusion' (line 696). In the city he cannot conjure up any of the sympathy which he feels towards a beggar encountered on a midnight walk in the country, as in Book IV, or that easy generalised love for villagers and their daily round of activities with which Book VIII begins. London in *The Prelude* is described as a stereotypical focus of wicked metropolitan ways. Wordsworth depicts the city as a striking contrast to the beneficence of Nature and the Lake District. Though he asserts that his contact with Nature has afforded him such stability that he can see some kind of harmony beyond the discord, his distaste for the city and its inhabitants makes this a bit unconvincing.

BOOK EIGHTH : RETROSPECT – LOVE OF NATURE LEADING TO LOVE OF
            MANKIND

A village fair – love of nature analysed again – shepherds – the effect of reading on his perception of Nature and people – the growth of his love of humanity

The annual village fair in a valley below Helvellyn is described with affection and respect*. Wordsworth once again thanks Nature for helping him triumph over the 'loathsome sights' (line 65) of the city, and teaching him brotherly love. Two memories of shepherds are recounted*, one seen as if in an island of mists, the other training his dog.

Wordsworth's home ground, he asserts, is more beautiful than any exotic paradise. Love and feeling has been engendered by 'the common beauty of the green earth / With the ordinary human interests' (lines 166–7).

He expresses his admiration for shepherds, whose occupation connects them with Nature. His shepherds are practical men, not the artificial kind that poets sing about. He tells the story of a shepherd and his son, looking for a lost sheep, and how the son was dangerously stranded on an island till he was rescued by his father. Other shepherds spring to mind, in different lands. The shepherd's seasonal tasks are described. One he saw seemed like a giant, his sheep like 'Greenland bears' (line 402). Because of his admiration for such people, the human form for him is 'the index of delight, / Of grace and honour, power and worthiness' (lines 415–16).

This pure form, in which he first encountered his fellow man, prepared him for the 'deformities of crowded life' (line 465). For a long time, though, his love of Nature was paramount.

He thinks of other kinds of workers. He describes how reading books gave him the habit of embroidering fancies around other people's lives and natural objects. A black rock in a copse near his home entranced and frightened him. But the 'real, solid world / Of images' (lines 604–5) brings him back to earth.

Later in his phase of rapturous pleasure in Nature, Man is correspondingly ennobled. The superficiality of his life in Cambridge had been succeeded by the labyrinth of London. Wordsworth analyses his perception of humanity in terms of the spirit and the unity of Nature. He remembers seeing a workman cradling a sick baby with 'unutterable love' (line 859). Through sights such as this he gradually came to love humanity.

> The misanthropic feelings generated by his stay in London are rectified when Wordsworth finds himself back in contact with Nature, and with rural people in the Lake District. Wordsworth's debate about his love of mankind can seem somewhat contrived. It is as if he senses an inadequacy in his horrified reaction to the city and its inhabitants, who of course are just as much a part of the 'nature' of things, considered from the broadest possible point of view, as country-dwellers. Certainly he feels that this aspect of his thinking requires his special examination and analysis, which is at the centre of this book.

> He puts forward shepherds as the best type of human being; they are purified, like himself, by constant contact with the elemental world of Nature. We may commend Wordsworth for his lack of snobbery in turning his back on 'society' – those worlds dealt with at many levels in the novels of the period. One of Wordsworth's shepherds would look very strange, for example, in a novel by Jane Austen.

It is perhaps easy to forget how much of a break Wordsworth was making with what his contemporaries might have expected from an ambitious writer, eager to be published. A ploughman poet, like Robert Burns, was acceptable and revered, perhaps as a kind of exotic. But Wordsworth was choosing to align himself with rural working people for themselves, not because they had chosen to become poets. He is anxious not to sentimentalise or glamorise his subject matter: these are working shepherds that he admires, not pastoral philosophers, as his anecdotes and stories show. The revolutionary programme of *Lyrical Ballads*, written and published during the period covered by *The Prelude*, was to forge a new subject matter and method for poetry, and Wordsworth's innovatory ideas and allegiances should not be underestimated, though we may find his expression of them too willed and awkwardly explicit. Assertion and repetition is an uncomfortable way of demonstrating a growing love for fellow human beings. (See also the discussion of Wordsworth and his Characters, pp. 112–14.)

B OOK NINTH: RESIDENCE IN FRANCE

> **Paris after the Revolution – friendship with a group of monarchist officers – the patriot Beaupuis – their discussions and walks – the tale of Vaudracour and Julia**

Wordsworth is pleased to feel the impulse to move his 'long work' on, much needed, as he is about 'ungenial' material (line 16).

After a year in London, he went again to France, to live in a city on the Loire, with the intention of improving his French. First he explored Paris, and saw as a tourist the aftermath of revolution.

To begin with he was absorbed by the intrinsic interest of being in a foreign country, and even avoided the political ferment. His chief associates were a group of officers intent on undoing the Revolution. Wordsworth describes how one of these men was physically broken by the unhealthy agitation of the times. They accepted Wordsworth and tried to bring him round to their cause, but he was constitutionally not interested in monarchism. Born in a poor district, and growing up in 'God and Nature's single sovereignty' (line 238) he thought best 'the government of equal rights / And individual worth' (lines 248–9), and Republicanism came naturally to him. The officers' arguments did not convince Wordsworth and, indeed, strengthened his political leanings.

Even now Wordsworth is moved to tears by memories of the shattering effects that the conflict had on ordinary people, yet it was a thrilling time. One of the officers, spurned by the others, was a patriot, a man of excellent and noble character, and with him Wordsworth enjoyed many political discussions in praise of 'a people risen up / Fresh as the morning star' (lines 392–3). Conversation about liberty was sweet, but it was even better to put such views into action: this man, Beaupuis, later died fighting for 'Liberty against deluded men' (line 433).

In the meantime the two of them walked in the woods, where Wordsworth often let his imagination run wild. **Romantic** visions of French history sometimes softened his Patriotic fervour, though his 'hatred of absolute rule, where will of One / Is law for all' (lines 504–5) was strengthened by the poverty they encounter.

Wordsworth tells the tale of Vaudracour and Julia (lines 556–935), two young lovers. She becomes pregnant, but they are split apart by their families' disapproval. Vaudracour's father was implacably against his son's liaison, and sends ruffians to attack him. Vaudracour kills one of them and is imprisoned. Released on pain of not seeing Julia, he visits her and is imprisoned again, and then released again, just before Julia gives birth. The father still would not condone their marriage, and Julia, in despair, joins a nunnery, leaving her baby in Vaudracour's care. He goes to live in the country with the child and a nurse, but, through some mistake, the baby dies. Vaudracour descends into silence, misery and madness.

> Wordsworth often works hard to give his poetry the appearance of authenticity, though sometimes his material may be fictional (see the discussion of 'The Solitary Reaper', pp. 43–7).

> Should autobiography tell the truth, or is it sufficient that it should appear to do so? Should it tell 'the whole truth'? Is such a thing as 'the whole truth' possible? If it is found out that autobiographical writers are omitting or concealing part of their life, does this render their writing invalid?

> Book IX concludes with the tale of Vaudracour and Julia, a modern version of the Romeo-and-Juliet situation of two lovers kept apart by

their parents, a situation compounded and complicated in this case by the birth of an illegitimate child. There seems no particular reason to tell this story – it does not demonstrate anything specific about revolutionary France and seems no more than a sentimental digression.

During his lifetime, only Wordsworth's closest friends knew that while in France he met and fell in love with a young woman, who gave birth to his child. This episode did not become public knowledge till 1922 when it was brought to light in a biographical study, *Wordsworth and Annette Vallon*, by Emile Legouis. The tale of Vaudracour and Julia is usually considered to be an oblique reference to this experience, a way perhaps of honouring or exorcising something that the poet felt unable to discuss openly for fear of stigma.

B OOK TENTH: RESIDENCE IN LONDON AND FRENCH REVOLUTION

Politics in France – in Paris again – return to England – Britain declares war on France – his torn feelings – the death of Robespierre – the thrill of being in revolutionary France remembered – all is now turned to shame and despair – Dorothy, Coleridge and Nature help him during this mental crisis

Wordsworth went to Paris, where the Republic had been declared. The massacres seemed to have finished, though he was fearful violence would return. Robespierre had been denounced. Wordsworth was agitated by the prospects of success for the Revolution, but still hoped that virtue would clear 'a passage for good government' (line 185).

Reluctantly he returned to England. Believing that success in France will put everything right, he was not interested in the fortunes of the anti-slavery movement. To his surprise Britain declared war on France. Torn by contrary feelings, he rejoiced when the English army is defeated, and viewed the English Fleet, anchored at the Isle of Wight, with pain. But in France the war allowed tyrants to take over, and 'domestic carnage' (line 329) ensued. Though France repelled the invaders, lamentable 'atrocities' (line 371) were committed, and Wordsworth found sleep difficult, disturbed by 'a sense / Of treachery and desertion in the place, / The holiest that I know of, my own soul' (lines 378–80).

Y

Sometimes the news from France still thrilled him. Visiting the grave of an old teacher, he met with a party of travellers*, who told him, to his delight, that Robespierre was dead. He looks back at the narrow-minded English view of French events at this time, and the way the English state undermined the liberty of its subjects. He remembers the fervour he felt for a revolution that would bring out the best in man: 'Bliss was it in that dawn to be alive' (line 692). But what had been a source of pride turned to shame at the news from France. He discusses the rational philosophy that used to excite him, though he asserts that he never thought ill of human kind. Trying by reason to work out his political and social opinions, he fails: 'sick, wearied out with contrarieties, / [he] Yielded up moral questions in despair' (lines 899–900). His sister and Coleridge helped him, and Nature too. The worst moment comes when: 'a Pope / is summon'd in to crown an Emperor ... the dog / Returning to his vomit' (lines 932–5). In a long address to Coleridge, he laments that his friend has gone to Sicily, but takes solace from imagining him there.

If Wordsworth is economical with the truth about his love affair in France, he is scrupulously honest about his feelings with regard to the French Revolution. This honesty encompasses a whole spectrum of emotions, from tremendous enthusiasm for the revolutionary cause, through a terrible sense of divided loyalty after the declaration of war against France, to the nadir of his misery at the eventual outcome of the Revolution, symbolised by the Pope crowning Napoleon Emperor in 1804. The despair that grew out of the crushing of all his beliefs and ideas led to a state of mind that in the next century might have been labelled a 'mental breakdown'. It is this desolation that triggers the therapeutic aspect of *The Prelude*: this is why he needs to fix the 'wavering balance' of his mind (Book I, 650). Ironically, the present-day reader is likely, on the one hand, to be disturbed and moralistic about Wordsworth's sexual dishonesty, and on the other hand surprised by the frankness and candour with which he describes the absolute collapse of his political, intellectual and spiritual values.

The Prelude, personal though it is, provides an account of the severe disillusionment of a generation of thinkers and writers. Many British intellectuals embraced the French Revolution, but few persevered in their faith after the Reign of Terror, the British declaration of war against the revolutionary army, and the rise of Napoleon, whose intention, amongst other things during the late 1790s, was to invade Britain. Wordsworth and many of his contemporaries had their intellectual beliefs shattered in the course of a few years by a succession of public events which rendered them traitors. The unpleasantness of this process should not be underestimated. Fearful of a revolution in Britain, in 1794 Pitt suspended Habeas Corpus and suppressed the freedom of the press. Political tension was extreme. Wordsworth and Coleridge were spied upon by government informers, who ludicrously reported that the two poets had been talking about a certain 'Spy Nosey' – a misapprehension of the philosopher Spinoza.

Book Eleventh: Imagination, How Impaired and Restored

Nature endures in spite of human perversity – the place of Reason in the development of his thought – the tyranny of the visual – benefits of a simple response to Nature – tribute to 'a maid' – the 'spots of time' – two examples

Wordsworth decides this is enough about 'utter loss of hope itself' (line 6); his poem did not start in this vein. The objects of Nature continue notwithstanding 'man's perverseness' (line 23); morning and spring continue to arrive.

He looks back on the war of ideas within himself, and how he became unable to connect his past with his present. Reason led him to distrust poetry and history, and even his pleasure in Nature was dominated by 'a taste / Less elevated' (lines 116–17). Reason, as a function, is better as 'the enemy of falsehood' than the 'friend of truth' (lines 135–7). It results in judgement at the expense of feeling. Sight – 'The most despotic of our senses' (line 178) – held dominion over his mind, and he sought combinations of things to look at that were vivid rather than profound. This behaviour Wordsworth contrasts with a 'Maid' who found contentment in 'whatever scene was present to her eyes' (line 208). Before he left his 'native hills' (line 225) he too had loved what was before him.

However the degradation was transient, because he had felt the 'visitings of imaginative power' (line 253) so early in life, and now once more he stands in Nature's power, 'a sensitive and creative soul' (line 257).

Wordsworth explains that there are 'spots of time' (line 258) to which the mind returns to repair itself when cast down by depression. These moments, scattered through childhood, are at times when the mind, rather than 'outward sense' (line 272), dominates. He describes one such memory*. By mischance he found himself alone in the eerie place where a murderer was hanged. Someone had carved the murderer's name on the turf. Thereafter he saw a pool, a beacon, and a girl who bears a pitcher on her head. The scene struck him with 'visionary dreariness' (line 311), but when he returns to it in later life, he feels pleasure and 'youth's golden gleam' (line 323). The depth of these feelings is a mystery to him, but so far he can still see glimpses, like this, of what he feels is the source of his power.

The second such incident* occurs while he was waiting impatiently for the horses which would take his brother and himself home for Christmas. He climbed up to a high point, where, with a stone wall, a sheep, and a hawthorn, he stared out into the mist. Soon after this his father died, and he guiltily associated this tragic event with his hopeful watching. Again this memory is something to which he constantly returns in his mind for some kind of sustenance.

Book XI contains what is in many respects the focus of Wordsworth's development of his philosophy. The writer William Godwin was amongst those radical English intellectuals who believed that Reason was the highest instrument of thought and principle of action, and that the French Revolution was the apotheosis of Reason. His *An Enquiry concerning Political Justice* (1793) argued for the rejection of law, religion, marriage and property. Wordsworth had been caught up by Godwin's ideas at the time of his support for the Revolution: as he puts it, he had been 'a Bigot to a new Idolatry' (line 75), who did 'zealously labour to cut off [his] heart / From all the sources of her former strength' (lines 77–8). He analyses the defects of a life built around Reason alone – a more balanced approach does not ignore the value of feeling as a guide to thought and behaviour.

In a strange passage he blames as particularly disturbing the dominance of the visual at one time in his life, a state he passed through in

HE PRELUDE: BOOKS III–XIII

which 'the eye was master of the heart' (line 172). Sight, 'the most despotic of our senses' (line 174), held his mind in 'absolute dominion' (line 176). He describes himself searching the countryside for ever more striking combinations of beautiful objects in his 'thraldom' to the 'empire' of the sight. 'Liberty' from this can only be gained from a more complete consideration of things, engaging the entire gamut of feeling. Throughout this discussion he uses the language of political domination: 'dominion', 'empire', 'thraldom'. Nature employs a means to 'thwart / This tyranny' (lines 79–80), though he chooses not to explain this. Wordsworth seems to realise how his worship of Nature could have become a sort of rural aestheticism, dominated only by the beautiful appearance of selected portions of the natural world, spacious panoramas, perhaps, or perfect views of mountains. Throughout his poetry he often shows a particular consciousness of *seeing*. In 'Tintern Abbey' he oddly states that what he sees again is 'not … as is a landscape to a blind man's eye', a curiously negative way of drawing attention to the value of sight. Earlier in *The Prelude* he describes how sometimes the world seen around him became internalised, so that he lost a sense of his 'bodily eyes' and it became a dreamlike 'prospect in my mind' (Book II, lines 369–71). But investigation of those stretches of poetry where he achieves his best effects suggest that they go beyond what is seen, to involve other senses, often hearing, and, more markedly, a whole gamut of feelings, ideas and memories. And Wordsworth is rarely a narrowly descriptive poet, in the sense of building a picture in words of his subject matter – his descriptions are always infused with figurative language, especially metaphors, establishing a particular way of perceiving an object. Examples of descriptive passages that demonstrate Wordsworth's typical methods can be found in the discussion of the boat-stealing incident in Book II (pp. 62–3) and the extended examination of his account of walking through the Alpine chasm (pp. 81–4).

In contrast with those times when he allowed seeing to dominate his response to things, he rather tritely extols the simplicity of response of a particular 'Maid' (Mary Hutchinson, whom he married in 1802). Wordsworth's depiction of women in *The Prelude* – Dorothy figures

most, Mary Hutchinson occasionally – is usually limited to this kind
of exaggerated praise, by which they are dehumanised and turned
into spirits or angels:

> God delights
> In such a being; for her common thoughts
> Are piety, her life in blessedness. (lines 221–3)

As another contrast to the tendency to allow his perception to be
dominated on the one hand by Reason, and on the other hand by the
beautiful appearance of things, he elaborates his idea of 'the spots of
time'. This is the culmination of Book XI, and indeed of several
strands of the whole poem: it brings together the therapeutic aspect
of his creative labours, the analysis of mind begun in the journey to
childhood through memory, and the growing understanding of the
value of feelings which he cannot explain through rational argument.
It also offers an implicit comment on the methods of the poem and
some of Wordsworth's other poetry.

A 'spot' of time is already a concept arrived at by metaphor, uniting
'spot', a concrete location with 'time', an abstraction (though until the
digital age the measurement of time had always had to be expressed
by spatial metaphors, of distance travelled, for example in the form of
the advancing shadow of a sundial, or the hands of a clock). The
handling of time is a basic problem in autobiographical writing, for
which there are many possible solutions. Wordsworth sticks more or
less to a chronological ordering of his narrative, broken up by
constant time-of-writing reflections. And, as noted in the critical
comment on Book VII, he makes the reader conscious that the time-
of-writing is also moving forward during the creation of the work:
the Wordsworth who began writing the poem years before is not the
same as the Wordsworth who writes at the end of the work, who has
come to terms with his two-fold experience, in the sense of the story
of his past and in the new knowledge acquired during the telling and
examination of that story. The 'spots of time' are the fruit of this
examination of himself.

In his effort to regain his mental balance after the breakdown of his
intellectual framework, he finds that the contemplation of a number

of vivid memories is in itself curative, though he admits he can find
no rational explanation for their power:

> There are in our existence spots of time,
> Which with distinct pre-eminence retain
> A vivifying Virtue, whence, depress'd
> By false opinion and contentious thought,
> Or aught of heavier or more deadly weight
> In trivial occupations, and the round
> Of ordinary intercourse, our minds
> Are nourish'd and invisibly repair'd,
> A virtue by which pleasure is enhanced
> That penetrates, enables us to mount
> When high, more high, and lifts us up when fallen.
> This efficacious spirit chiefly lurks
> Among those passages of life in which
> We have had deepest feeling that the mind
> Is lord and master, and that outward sense
> Is but the obedient servant of her will. (lines 258–73)

Words such as 'intercourse' and 'penetrate' are now commonly used
with reference to sexual activity, and this tends to draw immediate
attention to the sexual aspect of the passage, colouring other words
such as 'pleasure' and 'mount'. Are sexual memories amongst those
that 'lurk' in Wordsworth's mind, sources of nourishment and repair?
Even more curious is the way that 'mind' changes gender, from 'lord
and master' to 'her will'.

Wordsworth relates two memories as illustration of his theory. One
is of a girl with a pitcher on her head, struggling against the wind, a
pool and a beacon. The other comprises a sheep, a thorn tree and a
stone wall. They are banal in themselves (though we should perhaps
wonder whether a young woman carrying a pitcher on a high and
desolate moor was a common sight, or was in itself somewhat
extraordinary). But Wordsworth shows clearly how in both incidents
his state of mind, for different reasons, was highly attuned and
receptive, and how this turned these moments into personal symbols,
filled in recollection with meaning and value. When recreated in

verse they show the whole mind engaging with the world and creating meaning from it. This is the natural capacity of the poetic imagination, which as the title of Book XI makes clear, can be and has been 'impaired' and 'restored'.

As usual Wordsworth gives thanks for the faculty, though here it is not Nature that he regards as the source, except in so far as the functioning of mind is 'natural':

> Oh! mystery of Man, from what a depth
> Proceed thy honours! I am lost
> But see in simple childhood something of the base
> On which thy greatness stands, but this I feel,
> That from thyself it is that thou must give,
> Else never canst receive. The days gone by
> Come back upon me from the dawn almost
> Of life: the hiding-places of my power
> Seem open; I approach, and then they close;
> I see by glimpses now. (lines 329–34)

Here the mind must 'give' before it can receive. In other words, it is the mind that must find order in the world around it; imagination is creative, not merely receptive. The emphasis of childhood in the discussion of the 'spots of time' – in childhood they are 'most conspicuous' (line 277) – harks back to the discussion of the infant's active perception of the world in Book II.

Throughout *The Prelude* 'spots of time', passages where an attempt is made to recreate a particular incident in all its detail of sense and feeling, are a means of ordering the narrative, and helping the narrative avoid what could have become a tendency towards arid abstraction. Wordsworth did not set out to write a book of philosophy; he believes that the wholeness of existence cannot be expressed via rational or philosophical or analytic discourse. Poetry is capable of dealing with the whole gamut of being and consciousness, in a way that other kinds of discourse cannot.

THE PRELUDE: BOOKS III–XIII

BOOK TWELFTH: THE SAME SUBJECT – CONTINUED

Nature continues to bestow its gifts on him – his walking habits – reflections on poverty and wealth – the chosen subject of his poetry – a reverie on Salisbury Plain

Both emotion and 'moods / Of calmness' (lines 2–3) are the gift of Nature. Everyone partakes of this beneficial agent, which provides the imaginative energy to grasp the world, and the peace of mind to receive information unsought. Wordsworth himself, under the good effect of Nature, regained his delight in humanity, and acquired a more sober knowledge of the world.

Growing sceptical of politicians and their ambitions, he has looked to see how much knowledge and power exists among labouring people.

Walking, especially with a loved one, is a particular happiness. 'The lonely roads / Were schools to me' in which to study 'the passions of mankind' (lines 163–5). There he met mad people and vagrants, yet what he learned from them was more valuable than formal education. Wordsworth discusses the bad effects of abject poverty, and on living in the city, on the growth of the emotions. But too often our judgements are formed through literature by an elite, 'the wealthy few' (line 208), who neglect 'the universal heart' (line 219).

Wordsworth reveres 'men as they are men within themselves' (line 225). He wants in his verse to take as its theme the best people, who live 'in Nature's presence' (line 244), though with the help of literature and religion. They may be articulate, or they may be incapable of the 'the strife of phrase' (line 267), but possess 'the language of the heavens, the power, / The thought, the image, and the silent joy' (lines 270–1). Nature can consecrate and bless even the most humble. Poets have the prophetic power, himself included he hopes, to see things that have not been understood before. He describes a reverie* that came to him on Salisbury Plain, of ancient Britain; he imagined both the fires of human sacrifice, and the music of the druids inscribing their astronomical knowledge in the mysterious mounds and lines that still survive. At that time Coleridge encouraged him to think he had insights that were worthy of expression, and he believes too that then in 'life's every-day appearances' he had 'sight / Of a new world ... fit / To be transmitted and made visible / To other eyes' (lines 369–73).

The penultimate book continues various strands of debate with which we are already familiar: the beneficial agency of Nature, Wordsworth's interest in the humble labouring classes, his passion for walking, what kinds of men are the appropriate subject for his poetry. There is a reverie of historical England, sparked off by seeing Stonehenge, which is different in kind from the other various dreams and visionary moments recounted in the poem. This is a *willed* fantasy; it does not come to him through the normal processes of memory selection, like a 'spot of time', nor is it a dream. It shows Wordsworth advancing his claim to be a prophetic poet, seeing and imagining beyond the surface of things, and he reminds Coleridge that he has encouraged him in this direction in the past. Wordsworth's poetical vastly serious ambitions as a poet and his explicit ruminations about his sense of his own value and worth, are never far from the main direction of his narrative.

BOOK THIRTEENTH: CONCLUSION

Climbing Snowdon – a strange panorama and its meaning – reflection on his experiences over all – Dorothy and Coleridge's support – tribute to his patron – hopes and ambitions as a poet

Wordsworth climbed Snowdon on a sultry summer's night*. Arriving above the clouds, he suddenly saw the moon above a sea of mist, with the tops of hills and the real sea beyond. Not far away was a 'blue chasm' (line 56), through which could be heard the roar of torrential waters below. This struck Wordsworth as 'The perfect image of a mighty Mind' (line 69), in its constant exchange between infinity and an 'underpresence' (line 71). Nature presented him with such a spectacle that it could not be ignored. He goes on to define the 'highest bliss' of the imaginative thinker, which is to have 'the consciousness / Of whom they are habitually infused / Through every image and through every thought / And all impressions' (lines 107–11).

Wordsworth believes through all these experiences he remained true to himself. He never allowed his mind to be enslaved by habit and thereby gave in to the 'universe of death' (line 138). In this endeavour his sister and

Coleridge both helped. His schooling trained him to be independent-minded. His 'Wanderer's life' (line 336) was allowed by the financial support of his friend Calvert.

Wordsworth wonders whether he will ever accomplish enough to justify 'this Record of myself' (line 382). He reminds Coleridge of the work they have shared, and hopes to see him soon, when they can together be 'Prophets of Nature' (line 435).

> The final book is dominated by a 'spot of time' that presents itself, or is presented by Nature to Wordsworth while climbing Snowdon. Such a scene cannot fail to impress itself upon the mind and memory, he argues, and he provides a set piece of poetic description of a vivid and arresting natural phenomenon. Walking though mist, he suddenly arrives above the cloud level, and is astonished by the moon high above a huge sea of mist, from which the surrounding hills 'their dusky backs upheaved' (line 45). The cloud-sea merges with the real sea in the distance. Not far away is a blue chasm:

> > ... a fracture in the vapour
> > A deep and gloomy breathing place thro' which
> > Mounted the roar of waters, torrents, streams
> > Innumerable, roaring with one voice. (lines 55–9)

> As so often, things of nature are given human elements; here inanimate noises of water are turned into a voice, while the sea of mist is 'meek and silent' (line 44). Stillness and activity, peace and noise, the clarity of the high moon contrasted with the wide amorphousness of the sea of cloud, these are some of the various opposite qualities that are brought into harmonious composition, by Nature and by Wordsworth.

> Wordsworth offers to interpret the landscape's symbolism. What he has seen is:

> > The perfect image of a mighty Mind,
> > Of one that feeds upon infinity,
> > That is exalted by an underpresence,
> > The sense of God, or whatso'er is dim
> > Or vast in its own being ... (lines 69–73)

'Underpresence' – one of the words that Wordsworth coins in his effort to analyse the workings of the mind – seems like a version of the subconscious or unconscious. He moves on quickly, leaving the reader to puzzle over this idea. Grammatically it is not clear exactly what is the 'perfect image' – the cloud chasm, the whole scene, or even the mountain? It is almost certainly the first of these possibilities that Wordsworth has in mind, but rather than teasing out an exact and clear explanation of his comment, the narrative moves on to a rapt equation of the workings of Nature with the imaginative function. Nature exerts her domination upon 'the outward face of things, / So moulds them, and endues, abstracts, combines' (lines 78–9), so that one object impresses above all others, in a way that even the 'grossest minds' (line 83) will recognise. Nature's method here – presumably to arrange the combination of mist, moon and cloud-chasm – is the exact counterpart of what 'higher minds' (line 90) do – which is to exercise the power of the imagination in all aspects of experience. Such people

> ... build up greatest things
> From least suggestions, ever on the watch,
> Willing to work and to be wrought upon,
> They need not extraordinary calls
> To rouze them, in a world of life they live,
> By sensible impressions not enthrall'd,
> But quicken'd, rouz'd, and made thereby more fit
> To hold communion with the invisible world. (lines 98–105)

The climax of this argument is a definition of the 'highest bliss' that such powerful persons can obtain:

> ... the consciousness
> Of whom they are habitually infused
> Through every image, and through every thought,
> And all impressions. (lines 108–11)

From this will spring religion, faith, cheerfulness, truth in moral judgements, and delight. Wordsworth himself, by implication, has knowledge of this exalted state, but, as the pattern of *The Prelude* has demonstrated, only intermittently, and he seems to feel his power is fading. Looking back to the cloud-chasm, from which Wordsworth has passed on, we may guess that what appealed to him was the ceaseless activity of its communication with 'infinity', everything that is going on, the 'underpresence', just as the perfectly working imaginative perception is in ceaseless contact with the individual's consciousness, with 'whom they are'. Understanding and acquiring a proper sense of the self has been the great aim and project of *The Prelude*, and the poet offers here a final, taxing paradigm, organised around a puzzling but powerful symbolic landscape.

PART THREE

CRITICAL APPROACHES

LYRICAL BALLADS AND THE 'PREFACE'

A collection of critical issues relate to this volume of poems, first published in 1798 and republished in 1800 with additions including a 'Preface' in which Wordsworth put forward a kind of credo about the nature of his poetry, that is an essential key to understanding (and misunderstanding) his intentions and beliefs as a poet.

Wordsworth and Coleridge had planned a joint volume while at Nether Stowey. It was to contain two kinds of poem, according to Coleridge in his account of the book's origins in Chapter XIV of *Biographia Literaria* (1817): in one kind, supernatural incidents were to be recounted along with the feelings of those who had experienced them as realities; the other kind would consist of incidents from ordinary life described so as to excite 'a feeling analogous to the supernatural, by awakening the mind's attention from the lethargy of custom'. Coleridge's was to contribute the first kind, which resulted in 'The Ancient Mariner'; Wordsworth was responsible for the second. The volume also contains poems like 'Lines, composed a few miles above Tintern Abbey...' which have nothing to do with these intentions. A second two-volume edition of *Lyrical Ballads* followed in 1800, with more poems and the famous 'Preface', and another in 1802 with the 'Preface' further expanded.

The title 'lyrical ballads' is something of a paradox in itself. The genres of 'lyric' and 'ballad' can be defined as in opposition to each other. A ballad is a narrative poem, usually presented from an anonymous point of view, and often related to the fate of characters in relation to public and historical events, such as war. A lyric is a poem about feelings, most often expressed by the poet as if personal and individual, and addressed to the reader in the manner of a private and intimate conversation. The title *Lyrical Ballads* thus brings together these two genres in an unexpected and potentially unusual way.

Though there were some readers who were immediately drawn to the kinds of poem there are in *Lyrical Ballads* and *Poems in Two Volumes* (1807) – the young De Quincey for example, who later was to seek

Wordsworth out and live in Dove Cottage – for several years they excited anger and contempt. A leading, vociferous, and acerbic critic was Francis Jeffrey writing in the *Edinburgh Review*, who constantly criticised what he called 'the fantastical oddity and puling childishness' of Wordsworth's poems, among others (this phrase is taken from his review of Crabbe's poems in 1808).

The 'Preface' is Wordsworth's first attempt to confront the unpopularity and anger that he seemed to know his poems could provoke. The *Lyrical Ballads*, he remarks, were 'an experiment'. A premise of his argument is that the volume consists of 'poems ... materially different from those upon which general approbation is at present bestowed', poems which might be read 'with a more than common dislike'. Wordsworth accepts (even provokes) the possibility that some readers will deny that his work is indeed 'poetry' at all:

> They who have been accustomed to the gaudiness and inane phraseology of many modern writers, if they persist in reading this book to its conclusion, will, no doubt, frequently have to struggle with feelings of strangeness and awkwardness: they will look round for poetry, and will be induced to inquire by what species of courtesy these attempts can be permitted to assume that title.

This is polemical writing, even a trifle melodramatic, in which Wordsworth places himself at odds with the contemporary state of poetry. The subject matter of his poems is also special, he implies:

> The principal object, then, proposed in these poems was to choose incidents and situations from common life, and to relate or describe them, throughout, as far as was possible in a selection of language really used by men, and, at the same time, to throw over them a certain colouring of imagination, whereby ordinary things should be presented to the mind in an unusual aspect ... Humble and rustic life was generally chosen, because, in that condition, the essential passions of the heart find a better soil in which they can attain their maturity ...

Wordsworth persevered in this belief through his poetic career. The discussion of shepherds in Book VIII of *The Prelude* argues this idea at length. Wordsworth also marks his poetry out for the refinement of feeling which it contains:

> It has been said that each of these poems has a purpose. Another circumstance distinguishes these poems from the popular poetry of the day; and it is this, that the

feeling therein gives importance to the action and the situation, and not the action and the situation to the feeling ... For a multitude of causes, unknown to former times, are now acting with a combined force to blunt the discriminating powers of the mind, and, unfitting it for all voluntary exertion, to reduce it to a state of almost savage torpor. The most effective of these causes are the great national events which are daily taking place, and the increasing accumulation of men in cities, where the uniformity of their occupations produces a craving for extraordinary incident, which the rapid communication of intelligence hourly gratifies.

Here Wordsworth appoints himself as the poet-guardian of true feeling in an urban society dominated by 'almost savage torpor'. The poet is a special person, at odds with the drift of humanity. Later on he defines the poet:

He is a man speaking to men: a man, it is true, endowed with more lively sensibility, more enthusiasm and tenderness, who has a greater knowledge of human nature, and a more comprehensive soul, than are supposed to be common amongst mankind.

His capacity to imagine and recreate his feelings is also greater than normal. Yet his language must often fall short of that 'uttered by men in real life'.

His most famous pronouncement on poetry in the 'Preface' concerns the poet's ability to reconstruct feeling:

I have said that poetry is the spontaneous overflow of powerful feelings: it takes its origin from emotion recollected in tranquillity: the emotion is contemplated till, by a species of reaction, the tranquillity gradually disappears, and an emotion, kindred to that which was before the subject of contemplation, is gradually produced, and does actually exist in the mind.

This comment applies chiefly to the conditions of composition, and for most of the poems in *Lyrical Ballads* it is not especially helpful in assisting our understanding. Nevertheless it often cited as the core explanation of Wordsworth's poetry, and it can certainly be applied usefully to those passages in *The Prelude*, where the verse recreates a memorable incident (the boat-stealing in Book II, for example, see pp. 62–3), in such a way that the reader is conscious of the poet's point of view both at the time of the experience and at the time of composition.

Wordsworth sets up an argument in the 'Preface' about the respective merits of science and poetry as a method of knowledge. The poet 'converses with general nature' while the scientist converses 'with those particular parts of nature which are the object of his studies'. Poetry will properly deal with scientific discoveries when they are 'familiar to us'. Meanwhile Wordsworth conveys in rapt and spectacular prose his high vision of the poet:

> Poetry is the breath and finer spirit of all knowledge; it is the impassioned expression which is in the countenance of all science. Emphatically it may be said of the poet, as Shakespeare has said of man, 'that he looks before and after'. He is the rock of defence for human nature; an upholder and preserver, carrying everywhere with him relationship and love. In spite of difference of soil and climate, and language and manners, of laws and customs: in spite of things gone silently out of mind, and things violently destroyed; the poet binds together by passion and knowledge the vast empire of human society, as it is spread over the whole earth, and over all time.

It is impossible to see how any of these tasks (and the list goes on) might be realised. This is Wordsworth's vision of universality, of which it is the poet's task, perhaps, to dream. As a contrast, here is W.H. Auden's view of what poetry can and cannot achieve, written just before the outbreak of the Second World War:

> For poetry makes nothing happen: it survives
> In the valley of its making where executives
> Would never want to tamper, flows on south
> From ranches of isolation and the busy griefs,
> Raw towns that we believe and die in; it survives,
> A way of happening, a mouth.

('In Memory of W.B.Yeats', 1940)

Auden connects poetry with isolation, survival, grief and belief; its voice suggests how we might live, but of itself, it does not make things happen.

POETIC DICTION

Wordsworth claims that *Lyrical Ballads* offers 'a selection of the language really used by men', a formulation that he repeats several times in his 'Preface'. This begs many questions: what does 'really' mean in this context? What kind of men does he mean? The implicit assumption is absurd: that there is a class or type of person that his readers will recognise as true 'men', whose use of language is somehow more 'real' than anyone else's. (And of course, as in all his writings, his use of the word 'men' – which he would have imagined included rather than excluded women – is now no longer permissible.) Wordsworth is taking up a position with regard to the appropriate language for poetry, and he wants a poetry that is plain in contrast with what he asserts is the prevailing taste of his time:

> There will also be found in these volumes little of what is usually called poetic diction; as much pains has been taken to avoid it as is ordinarily taken to produce it.

Poetic diction is that kind of ornate, elevated, and stilted figurative writing that some poets of the eighteenth century used. Later in the 'Preface' Wordsworth quotes a poem by Gray as an example of this kind of 'inane phraseology':

> In vain to me the smiling mornings shine,
> And reddening Phœbus lifts his golden fire:
> The birds in vain their amorous descant join,
> Or cheerful fields resume their green attire,
> These ears, alas! for other notes repine.

Thus the sun rising is 'reddening Phœbus lifts his golden fire', while the song of birds becomes 'amorous descant'. Gray wishes to adorn simple ideas with extravagant but conventional metaphors. In further quotations from this poem Wordsworth shows how Gray's best lines are the simplest, those which most resemble the plainness of prose, rather than aspiring to poetry through ornate diction and figurative language.

Wordsworth also abjures personification in the 'Preface' (for example, Phœbus – though the sun is not an abstraction):

> The reader will find that personifications of abstract ideas rarely occur in these volumes; and are utterly rejected, as an ordinary device to elevate the style, and raise it above prose. My purpose was to imitate, and as, as far as possible, to adopt the very language of men.

Of course it is very easy to find examples of Wordsworth not sticking to his own rules about the language of poetry, either in *Lyrical Ballads*, or in his later work. Nature is commonly personified in *The Prelude*, for example. However, his language is far plainer than the examples he cites from Gray. The diction of *Lyrical Ballads* is neither colloquial, nor in any way demotic (compare Larkin's 'They fuck you up, your mud and dad, / They don't mean to do it, but they do'), but it is, in relative terms, plain and simple. It is not 'the language really used by men'. It is written in metre, and it rhymes: a large part of the 'Preface' is devoted to explaining why the use of metre might not be an anomaly so far as the main argument is concerned. Coleridge refutes Wordsworth's arguments about metre and diction in Chapter XVIII of *Biographia Literaria*. Wordsworth's espousal of plain writing, 'the language really used by men', much vaunted in the 'Preface', is part of his polemical stance in *Lyrical Ballads*, and as a political gesture, in alliance with his dedication to 'humble and rustic life', it had consequences for the reception of the volume, at a time when most of the reading public, mindful of the Paris mob, was reacting strongly against ideas about the wisdom of 'the people' (see Literary Background).

NATURE AND PANTHEISM

'Nature' is a slippery concept, with a variety of meanings. In its widest definition it constitutes everything that there is around us, the universe, including cities and other physical structures that man has added to the planet's resources. 'Human nature' encompasses all kinds of behaviour, from the best to the worst. 'Nature' in the sense of the countryside, as opposed to the city, includes fields and farm land, hedges, copses, woods, all of which are either created or modified by human activity. The countryside of England in particular is almost all man-made, and in a sense artificial; it is the result of several millennia of agricultural activities of many kinds. Scotland and Wales include more areas of wilderness, including mountains, lakes, even a few remnants of ancient forest. These objects are more 'natural', more truly 'Nature' than farm land, perhaps. Wordsworth's beloved Lake District contains more wilderness of this kind than most of England; it is a mixture of farmland and wild nature – but in the wildest spots sheep still wander and feed, and there are few if any vantage points where one can look out on a landscape that has completely escaped the impression of man. Wordsworth likes the wilderness landscape, the crags, rocks, lakes and mountains of his Lake District. But he also likes the villages, cottages, country roads, all the signs of country living that go on in the proximity of the wilderness. He prefers not to think about large conglomerations of humanity in the city, as we learn in Book VII of *The Prelude*. In *Michael*, when Luke goes off to the city, his falling into wickedness seems like a foregone conclusion – it requires no explanation.

The industrial revolution is conventionally thought of as covering the period from 1740 to 1850. Wordsworth could not be unaware that his lifetime coincided with the huge growth of cities and the development of a new urban working class. Yet the London Wordsworth describes is not an industrial city, and his northern England does not encompass Manchester and Leeds. The Spinning Jenny, which allowed one person to spin several threads, was invented in 1764; it spelled the end of spinning as a cottage industry. Five years later Watt perfected the steam engine, which was to power the mills and pump the mines of industrial Britain. This new world barely impinges on Wordsworth's poetry, except in the way his work often seems implicitly to lament the passing of another better age, of childhood and youth often, but also the age in which the old men he admires grew up.

Wordsworth's choosing to live in the Lake District, and making its inhabitants and landscape a central and distinguishing feature of his poetry, it may be inferred, is a reaction against the industrial revolution, and against the burgeoning cities. So 'normal' does it seem in our day to *escape* to the wildernesses of Britain, or other less tame wildernesses far away, that it is difficult to see how peculiar this aspect of our culture is. Eighteenth-century European society re-invented the countryside as a *locus* for beauty and holiday, rather than the antithesis of society, a place of ignorance, dullness and possibly danger.

Wordsworth inscribed his vision of Nature into English literature, but it is not a 'natural' vision. For St Augustine, heaven was the 'City of God'. The city is a dwelling place carved from the sterile wilderness, an image of human civilisation. Dr Johnson (1709–84) famously remarked that 'When a man is tired of London, he is tired of life'. But for Wordsworth 'Nature' – his Lake District – is the place where humankind is at its best – not the city.

By Nature Wordsworth can mean any number of a variety of different things. Firstly it is the landscape of the Lake District, combining pastoral and agricultural land, trees and flowers, and the wilderness of the surrounding mountains (or similar natural features if experienced, say, in the Wye Valley). Secondly it is such a landscape in time, subjected to the recurring cycles of summer and winter, growth and decay, birth and death, of which country dwellers are constantly aware because their labours have to coexist with the rhythm of the seasons. Thirdly it is the landscape conceived as enduring outside time, and thereby offering an image of the eternal. (Mountains are not strictly speaking eternal, but they last a long time; even trees commonly outlive humans.) Fourthly it is the universe of sky, oceans, stars, more images of endurance and eternity, not necessarily always visible to the eye, unlike the landscape, but present in the imagination. Fifthly it is the entire world of things, everything outside the self. Sixthly it is occasionally a personification, an abstract entity, but also a teacher and a nurse, that leads the boy Wordsworth on and educates him. What exactly is personified is not perfectly clear or consistent. However, this Nature forces him to be aware – and the young Wordsworth is often too self-absorbed to remember this – that the world outside his imagination exists, containing things he does not understand, things that frighten him unexpectedly, 'unknown modes of being', symbols of eternity and otherness. All these various versions of Nature move in and out of each other in Wordsworth's poetry.

As is described in the commentaries on several of his poems, Wordsworth is not simply a descriptive poet – his accounts of Nature can offer many different experiences. They may be simply a background for human action, a method of self-analysis, a commentary of the functioning of the imagination, an exploration of the re-creative powers of language, or an opportunity to discover and create symbols of eternity. Nature is the source and subject of all these processes in *The Prelude*.

Nature is also the source of a kind of religion. Wordsworth's early poems are surprisingly a-religious. In 'Michael', the protagonist seems the type of human excellence for Wordsworth, but there is no mention of his going to church; work, thrift and honesty are enough (or is church-going taken for granted?). It is odd that in *The Prelude* there is almost no attention to formal religion; again, there is almost no church going (a drunken and tardy rush to chapel in Cambridge), and no accounts of institutional worship, or, indeed, of orthodox belief. That long poem is a quest that is involved with Wordsworth's soul – he uses the word often. He is re-discovering his confidence in himself and in humanity, and this has a moral and spiritual dimension. Nature, as he argues throughout, helps him in this aim. It is not an easy process, but has to be achieved. In so far as the poem expresses faith, it is one that works through encounters and intuitions, and has to be discovered and tested.

'Tintern Abbey', which looks forwards in many respects to *The Prelude*, is also a meditation in *process*. Critics often remark on Wordsworth's pantheistic beliefs in this poem and others. Pantheism is the doctrine that the divine encompasses everything, and man and Nature are not independent of God. Wordsworth seems to be discovering a pantheistic vision when in his meditation he encounters the 'something far more deeply interfused' that 'rolls through all things'. *The Prelude* extends similar arguments at some of its great moments of intuition, such as for example the account of the Alpine chasm in Book VI: man is part of Nature, and all is divine. But in so far as Wordsworth is a pantheist, this is a position that he discovers in the course of the poem, rather than a set of beliefs that he states as certainties. And simply to attach the label 'pantheism' to 'Tintern Abbey', without a sense of the tentative, even tortuous way in which the argument moves forward, is to miss the whole point of the poem.

Pantheism is in many respects close to atheism; it denies that the boundary between God and man exist. As Wordsworth grew older he lost the tentative, exploratory attitude to ideas that characterised his earlier poems, and turned to orthodox religious positions. Gradually his poems rely on his perception of the eternal in Nature as a received truth. The nineteenth-century Wordsworthians admired this later religious poetry for its certitudes. Matthew Arnold (in his introduction to the *Poems* of 1879) was the first critic to point out that such verse was by no means 'a sweet union of philosophy and poetry', but bad poetry. He cites a passage from *The Excursion* as the centre of Wordsworth's ethical system (IV, lines 10–17):

> One adequate support
> For the calamities of mortal life
> Exists, one only; – an assured belief
> That the procession of our fate, howe'er
> Sad or disturbed, is ordered by a Being
> Of infinite benevolence and power;
> Whose everlasting purposes embrace
> All accidents, converting them to good.

For Arnold, this may be true doctrine, but it has 'none of the characters of *poetic* truth, which we require from a poet, and in which Wordsworth is really strong'.

There is another version of Nature that does not appear in Wordsworth's poetry, though the intimation of it may hover behind some of the moments of misery that so commonly give rise to his strivings for belief. This is Nature as a waste land without meaning, a world of predators red in tooth and claw, where there is no providential benevolence, no consolation. Arnold himself imagined such a Nature deprived of faith and God in 'Dover Beach' (1867):

> ... the world, which seems
> To lie before us like a land of dreams,
> So various, so beautiful, so new,
> Hath really neither joy, nor love, nor light,
> Nor certitude, nor peace, nor help for pain ...

WORDSWORTH AND HIS CHARACTERS

Tramps, beggars, an idiot boy, the weak, the poverty-stricken, and the insane: these are the characters of some of Wordsworth's early poems. In the 'Preface' he argues that in the rural poor 'the essential passions of the heart find a better soil in which they can attain their maturity' (see pp. 103–6). He places at the centre of his poetic vision types of people who are on the very margins of society. Shepherds are emblems for him of the same truth about 'essential passions', through constant contact with the seasons and the permanent forms of Nature, as he argues in Book VIII of *The Prelude*. They are the proper subject of his poetry, and the key to learning once more to love mankind, to overcome the misanthropy that resulted from his experiences in society, in France and London.

Tintern Abbey – a building not actually described in the poem called by that name – when Wordsworth looked at the picturesque Wye Valley, was apparently a refuge for beggars and tramps, yet in spite of his professed sympathies for such people, he does not mention this in the poem. They were not part of the famously beautiful landscape that Wordsworth had sought out for a second time. But anyway, *groups* of beggars are not part of his poetry's chosen subject matter; such people, when Wordsworth meets

Y

them, are always on their own, and so is he. Wordsworth does not like crowds. London he found a terrifying spectacle.

In his poetry Wordsworth is almost always remarkably solitudinous. At the end of 'Tintern Abbey' is a surprise when he turns from the meditation that he has shared with the reader and speaks to Dorothy. When he comes across the destitute soldier in Book IV of *The Prelude*, or the leech-gatherer in 'Resolution and Independence', it is the shock of encountering them unexpectedly that rouses him to thought. They, too, are solitudinous. His instinctive reaction in the imagined meeting in 'The Solitary Reaper' is 'Stop here! or gently pass'; he is alone, and it seems quite right to him to leave her alone.

Compared with his interest in the solitary, there is comparatively little sense in Wordsworth's poetry of villages or families or supporting social groups: In *Michael*, the household is three, then two when his son leaves, and they live outside the village (though Luke does say goodbye to his neighbours when he leaves). The rowdy gang of boys in the opening books of *The Prelude* is an exception, but the most interesting events happen to Wordsworth when he skates away from the crowd, or goes poaching or boat-stealing on his own.

There is something more than a trifle misanthropic about the 'self-sufficing power of solitude' which Wordsworth professes. The idea that humans are more completely human on their own, communing with Nature, is intrinsically antisocial. And the implicit message that true human contact is restricted to meetings between two persons, often occurring by chance, is also antisocial. For a man surrounded during much of his life by family and friends, there is surprisingly little sense of the value of human relations in his verse. We learn nothing of his travelling companion on the Continent. Coleridge and Dorothy and Mary Hutchinson are mentioned in *The Prelude*, but they are not created as characters. Even though the poem is addressed to Coleridge, the narrator seems always alone. Coleridge himself wrote with easy generosity about friendship in 'This Lime-Tree Bower My Prison', and in 'Frost at Midnight' he describes the pleasure of hearing his baby breathing by his side as he thinks about his past, and his child's future. Wordsworth's best love poems are about loss: the Lucy epitaphs and 'Surprised by Joy'.

Wordsworth's *forte* is what Keats called 'the wordsworthian or egotistical sublime': the main character in his poetry after *Lyrical Ballads* is himself. Although it is impossible to write about the self without constructing some kind of fiction, a **persona** or mask, the Wordsworth we encounter in the confessional or autobiographical poetry is surprisingly empty of individuating features, notwithstanding the great variety of things that happen to him. He is aware of the disparity between childhood memory and adult point of view, but he rarely views himself wryly or sentimentally, or ironically. Irony would only be possible if he shared a common point of view with his reader about what was ridiculous or false. But there is no sense of an agreed set of values with his reader, that would allow him to adopt an easier tone. How different it is from the narrator of a novel, who shows us a set of events from a recognisable point of view: we trust that he knows exactly what will happen as the plot unfolds.

Wordsworth is intensely serious. He is trying to discover who he is. It is as if every idea and opinion has to be argued from scratch, in the effort to reconstruct his vision of the world. The result is a surprisingly open encounter, for a remarkably sustained period, with a naked psyche, an honest self-absorption. There is a profound truth in this ultimate lack of knowledge about ourselves, except in terms of the events which define us. In Book III of *The Prelude* Wordsworth explores the impossibility of knowing his 'own heart', which is his 'heroic argument':

> It lies far hidden from the reach of words.
> Points have we all of us within our souls
> Where all stand single; this I feel, and make
> Breathings for incommunicable powers.
> Yet each man is a memory to himself... (lines 185–9)

It is this sense of the indefinableness and the loneliness at the heart of human consciousness that makes Wordsworth's sensibility so modern.

Part four

Background

Wordsworth's life

William Wordsworth was born in 1770 in Cockermouth, a small market town on the north west edge of the Lake District, some seven miles from the sea. He was the second child of five, born to Ann Wordsworth, the daughter of a draper from Penrith, and John Wordsworth, a lawyer who worked as the land agent and steward for the wealthy and corrupt local land-owner and politician, Sir John Lowther, Earl of Lonsdale. The seven Wordsworths lived in a large house supplied by Lowther, though they stayed frequently with their grandparents in Penrith.

Wordsworth went to a dame school in Penrith, and then to Cockermouth Grammar School. When he was not quite eight his mother died of tuberculosis, after which event Dorothy, Wordsworth's only sister and twenty months younger than him, was sent away to live with cousins, while the two oldest boys, Richard and William, went to Hawkshead Grammar School. They both lodged with a local couple, the Tysons; Wordsworth describes his fondness for Ann Tyson in *The Prelude*. The first two books also provide a vivid account of his boyhood activities. Once his school day was over, and during the holidays, he enjoyed absolute freedom to do exactly what he wanted. In 1783, when Wordsworth was thirteen, his father died.

In 1787 Wordsworth became a student at St John's College, Cambridge, where he ignored formal study, read English poetry and started to learn Italian. In 1789 he spent the Long Vacation with Dorothy and a young woman who had been at his first school, Mary Hutchinson. In 1790 he and a friend called Robert Jones walked through France and Switzerland across the Alps to Italy and back. After graduating, the two of them walked through North Wales to the Wye Valley, areas celebrated for their scenery. Later in 1791 Wordsworth went to France to live in Orleans and learn French. Though Wordsworth was an enthusiast for the revolutionary cause, he mixed with royalist sympathisers. He also met and fell in love with Annette Vallon. He was twenty-one, she was twenty-six. Their daughter Caroline was born in 1792, and in the same year

Wordsworth returned to England. Wordsworth did not attempt to hide his scandalous relationship, and his uncle withdrew the offer of financial support to help him become a clergyman in the Church of England.

France was declared a Republic in the same year. The massacre of the aristocracy culminated in the execution of Louis XVI in 1793 when Robespierre also began his reign of terror. England and France were at war. Wordsworth had to give up hopes of marrying Annette, though he saw her and his daughter again on several occasions, and they remained on good terms.

In 1795 his financial situation was helped, if not solved, by a bequest of £900 left him by Raisley Calvert, the brother of a school friend from Hawkshead. Dorothy and Wordsworth went to live in Racedown, Dorset. Meanwhile he was creating a reputation as a poet. He had met other poets, like Coleridge and Southey, and a publisher called Cottle. In 1797 Dorothy and he moved to live in Somerset to be near Nether Stowey where Coleridge was living. The two poets planned their joint volume, *Lyrical Ballads*. In 1798 Wordsworth revisited the Wye Valley with Dorothy, a visit which gave rise to the famous 'Lines written a few miles above Tintern Abbey' which was included in *Lyrical Ballads* and which was published anonymously with the help of Cottle in 1798.

After a brief stay in Germany, in 1799 Wordsworth and Dorothy moved to Dove Cottage in Grasmere, the first of the three houses which he was to inhabit in the Lake District. Eight happy and productive years followed, with a second book added to the *Lyrical Ballads*, which went through several editions. *Poems in Two Volumes* was published in 1807, and the thirteen book version of *The Prelude* was finished. Wordsworth also married Mary Hutchinson, and they had three children between 1803 and 1806. Dorothy's vivid and fascinating journals cover these years at Dove Cottage. For three years from 1808 to 1811 they lived at Allan Bank, where two more children were born (though two of the Wordsworths' children died during this period). In 1813 they moved to Rydal Mount, between Ambleside and Grasmere, where he was to live until his death.

In 1814 he published a long poem, *The Excursion*. Other volumes of verse followed, though none of the calibre of his first two collections. His reputation grew steadily from the 1820s, and tourists thronged to see the 'sage of Rydal' at home. Sometimes there were as many as thirty visitors a day, who might be charged for tea. Wordsworth was apt to reward them with lengthy speeches about his poetry and views. When Keats visited him in London in 1817, the young poet tried to intervene during one of Wordsworth perorations; Mary Wordsworth laid a hand on his arm and whispered 'Mr Wordsworth is never interrupted'.

As well as visits to London, there were continental tours. In 1820 Mary Wordsworth was taken to France, where she met Annette and Caroline Vallon. In the late 1830s the poet received two honorary doctorates, one from Durham University, the other from Oxford, where the event was met with 'thunders of applause, repeated over and over'. In 1843 he was made Poet Laureate, succeeding Southey. He died in 1850.

After the death of their father, the young Wordsworths had been looked after by their mother's father and brothers, who also took on their financial affairs, not least the legal battle to extract from the Earl of Lonsdale the huge sum of money he owed to the estate of John Wordsworth. The orphans did not enjoy this dependence on their dour maternal grandfather, and the small bequest that allowed William and Dorothy their financial independence was very welcome. In 1813 the Earl of Lonsdale died, and, partly in recompense for his father's financial malpractice, the new Lord Lonsdale appointed William Wordsworth to be Distributor of Stamps for Westmorland. The small but reliable income of between £400 and £600 per year from this civil service post gave Wordsworth his financial independence, much to the contempt of some of his fellow poets: 'Just for a handful of silver he left us', wrote Browning in 'The Lost Leader'.

Possibly as an effect of his own autobiographical stance in *The Prelude*, Wordsworth's life seems to have all its excitements crammed into his early years: the glorious freedoms of childhood, his walking tours, and his adventure into revolutionary France. One aspect of his youthful experience – perhaps not unusual for the time – prevailed during his maturity: the deaths of those closest to him. In 1805 his favourite brother was lost at sea. Three of his five children died during his lifetime: Catherine and Thomas in 1812, and Dora in 1841. Coleridge died in 1834 – though they had been estranged for a long time, their friendship is enshrined in *The Prelude* – and Annette Vallon in 1841. His beloved sister Dorothy, whose 'wild eyes' he described in 'Tintern Abbey', lived till 1855, but for the last twenty years of her life she was incapacitated by mental illness.

Wordsworth possessed a consistent and lively ambition to be a poet, which began in his schooldays and informed all his friendships and decisions. He was fully conscious of himself as an English poet, writing within a poetic tradition, both with a long history and a busy contemporary context, and which he seeks to modify and redirect by his own contribution. However, such self-consciousness does not necessarily make it easy to categorise the nature of this contribution, not least because there is a propagandist element in Wordsworth's early poetry and critical writing which both illuminates and obscures his position. Moreover, the developing variety of Wordsworth's verse along with his changing political and social views makes it difficult to tie him down to any simple pattern of influences and styles.

A key text in formulating Wordsworth's literary background is his 'Preface' to the second edition of *Lyrical Ballads*, in which he discusses the matter explicitly. Aspects of this text, and his rejection of poetic diction, are examined separately section (See Part Three, Poetic Diction). In choosing to call his poems 'ballads', Wordsworth was harking back to a key text of the late eighteenth century, Thomas Percy's *Reliques of Ancient English Poetry* (1765), the first major collection of popular ballads. In calling his poems 'ballads', and putting forward the arguments of his 'Preface', that the language of poetry should be that of the common man, and that human nature finds its perfect examples amongst the rural poor, Wordsworth was declaring his political allegiance to the ordinary people rather than the ruling classes. This espousal of populism was somewhat old-fashioned: it allied him with the neo-classicism of the eighteenth-century Enlightenment, the movement built on rationalism allied with notions of human perfectibility which was the background to the French Revolution. In spite of its populist message, it was also likely to be unpopular. The rural poor did not read poetry, Burns notwithstanding. Wordsworth's readership was composed of middle class intellectuals like himself. Many of his contemporaries had already moved away both from supporting the revolution, and a generalised admiration for the people. With Britain in conflict with revolutionary France, Wordsworth was openly adopting a risky position. The mob in Britain had sided with Church and King from early on – rioters attacked the homes of Dissenters in Birmingham in 1791 – but at the turn of the century British society was still in fear of insurrection within, and invasion from France. The mood of the reading public was strongly against populism. It seems to have been political conservatism – anti-populism – rather than poetics that fuelled the attacks on *Lyrical Ballads* by Jeffrey, the leading critic of the day, and even Coleridge's criticisms.

Though in his 'Preface' Wordsworth appears to be offering new and unusual subject matter, poetry about rural life had been common in the last quarter of the eighteenth century, as for example Goldsmith's *The Deserted Village* (1770), or Crabbe's *The Village* (1783). So even in his choice of material, Wordsworth's stance in the *Lyrical Ballads* is a strange mixture of the old-fashioned and the controversial.

In an 'Essay supplementary to the Preface of 1815' Wordsworth discusses poetry, religion and literary taste without the polemics of the earlier 'Preface', and offers a much clearer delineation of his formative reading. He criticises Pope, Johnson, Collins and Gray, and praises Percy's ballads, Burns, and James Thomson, whose long poems about the changing year in the countryside were brought together as *The Seasons* in 1730. His praise for Thomson is a reminder that the taste for landscape poetry was well established early in the eighteenth century. The meditative poem, in which a poet looks at landscape and has moral reflections, was brought to one kind of perfection by Gray in his 'Elegy written in a Country Churchyard' (1751), in which 'The ploughman homeward plods his weary way', though the description of landscape is far outweighed by abstractions and aphorisms. Nevertheless, it makes a useful contrast with 'Tintern Abbey', in which Wordsworth finds a quite different voice from that of the other *Lyrical Ballads*, but one which still has its precursors in the eighteenth century. In his use of blank verse, Wordsworth looks back past the eighteenth century to Shakespeare and Milton; and the influence of Milton particularly is marked in his later writing in this mode.

If there is little in Wordsworth's poetry that is entirely without antecedent (except perhaps the intense autobiographical self-analysis of 'Tintern Abbey' and *The Prelude*), what makes it special is the excellence of his writing. With few exceptions, Wordsworth's best work was all written before 1810, while it was generally reviled by all but a few admirers. From then onwards his verse became progressively duller and more dutiful, while ironically his reputation changed for the better. From about 1820 onwards, though he still had some detractors, he was widely read and admired. From then on his poetic output, as well as what other poets and critics thought about it, becomes part of the history of English poetry and criticism.

PART FIVE

CRITICAL HISTORY

WORDSWORTH AND THE CRITICS

Jeffrey's attacks on Wordsworth in the *Edinburgh Review* may have been politically motivated (see his comments on 'The Thorn' on p. 18 and on *Lyrical Ballads* on p. 104) – indeed in private he found Wordsworth's poetry moving – but there have always been readers who disliked or despised Wordsworth's verse for itself. During his lifetime and since, Wordsworth's writing has become what critics in the last years of the twentieth century called a 'site' for contestation and discussion.

Coleridge's discussion of Wordsworth in Chapters XIV–XXII of *Biographia Literaria* (1817) was a pioneering work in critical writing, a new kind of prose, still very much worth reading as a commentary on the nature of poetry and criticism. Other fellow poets were less reflective. Byron takes several swipes at Wordsworth. The following typifies his brusque rejection of almost all Wordsworth's stated intentions in *Lyrical Ballads*:

> That mild apostate from poetic rule,
> The simple Wordsworth …
> Who both by precept and example, shows
> That prose is verse, and verse is merely prose;
> Convincing all, by demonstration plain,
>
> Poetic souls delight in prose insane;
> And Christmas stories tortured into rhyme
> Contain the essence of the true sublime.
> Thus when he tells the tale of Betty Foy,
> The idiot mother of 'an idiot boy';
> A moonstruck silly lad, who lost his way,
> And, like his bard, confounded night and day;
> So close on each pathetic part he dwells,
> And each adventure so sublimely tells,
> That all who view the 'idiot in his glory'
> Conceive the bard the hero of the story.

(*English Bards and Scotch Reviewers*, 1809)

Shelley's sonnet 'To Wordsworth' (1816) gives credit for the bravery of Wordsworth's early career, but sorrows at his apostasy from liberty and lapse into conservatism, but his 'Peter Bell the Third' (1819) is less kind, mocking Wordsworth by parody and direct attack. Two stanzas will have to suffice:

> He had as much imagination
> As a pint pot; – he never could
> Fancy a situation
> From which to dart his contemplation
> Than that wherein he stood ...
>
> But from the first 'twas Peter's drift
> To be a kind of moral eunuch,
> He touched the hem of Nature's shift,
> Felt faint – and never dared uplift
> The closest, all-concealing tunic.

Keats, while admiring much in Wordsworth's verse, coined the phrase 'egotistical sublime' to define the opposite of what he felt to be a truer poetic talent for chameleon-like non-identity (Letter to Richard Woodhouse, 27 October 1818).

All this mockery and criticism by Wordsworth's contemporaries did not halt his growing popularity. Indeed that he became the target of so many of his fellow writers is, paradoxically, a clear demonstration of his growing consequence as a leading poet of the day.

Attacks on Wordsworth have often taken the form of parody, poking fun at his intense seriousness and lack of humour. An early draft of Lewis Carroll's 'White Knight' parodies 'Resolution and Independence' and draws attention to Wordsworth's egotistical complacence:

> I met an aged, aged man
> Upon the lonely moor:
> I knew I was a gentleman,
> And he was but a boor ...
>
> I did not hear a word he said,
> But kicked the old man calm,
> And said, 'Come, tell me how you live!'
> And pinched him on the arm.

Such a skit bounces harmlessly off the poem, but a later, more direct attack by J.K. Stephen identifies some of Wordsworth's lurching capacity to mix the potentially banal with the portentous:

Two voices are there: one is of the deep;
It learns the storm-cloud's thunderous melody,
Now roars, now murmurs with the changing sea,
Now bird-like pipes, now closes soft in sleep:
And one is of an old half-witted sheep
Which bleats articulate monotony,
And indicates that two and one are three,
That grass is green, lakes damp, and mountains steep
And Wordsworth, both are thine. (*Lapsus Calami*, 1891)

The orthodox Victorian view was to ignore the 'old half-witted sheep' and listen to the 'deep' Wordsworth. Compilations and critical works that demonstrated the 'wisdom', 'truth' and 'passion' of Wordsworth's verse were common. His own strange thematic organisation of his poems, under topics such as 'Poems of Fancy', 'Poems of Sentiment and Reflexion' perhaps helped to validate this approach. Wordsworth's poetry was valued for its power to heal and console, and as religious verse. It was also admired for its portrayal of human emotion, showing people how to feel, and how to manage their feelings. This is what the philosopher J.S. Mill found so valuable (see p. 8). Wordsworth's poetry becomes a kind of religion itself.

Every critic of note in the nineteenth century puzzled over the strangely mixed inheritance of Wordsworth's 'two voices'. Matthew Arnold's introduction to *Poems of Wordsworth* (1879) places the poet alongside Shakespeare, Molière, Milton and Goethe, yet agonises that 'pieces of high merit are mingled with a mass of pieces very inferior to them, so inferior to them that it seems wonderful how the same poet should have produced both':

To be recognized far and wide as a great poet, to be possible and receivable as a classic, Wordsworth needs to be relieved of a great deal of the poetical baggage which now encumbers him.

Arnold criticises the late poems as pious doctrine rather than poetry. They are 'a tissue of elevated but abstract verbiage'. He seeks to release the poet from the Wordsworthians who build an elaborate system of thought out of the poems, and thereby distort them: 'we cannot do him justice until we dismiss his formal philosophy'. His criterion for evaluating Wordsworth is put forward in a famous if somewhat vague assertion:

> It is important, therefore, to hold fast to this: that poetry is at bottom a criticism of
> life; that the greatness of a poet lies in his powerful and beautiful application of ideas
> to life, – to the question: How to live.

Wordsworth deals more powerfully with '*life*', Arnold argues, than other writers, and yet his praise is restricted to a handful of poems.

Throughout the twentieth century this puzzlement continued. Since 1850 many hundreds of books and articles have been written about Wordsworth, from almost every point of view imaginable, from his talents as a gardener, to interpretations of his verse in the light of **Queer Theory**. It is only possible to offer a sketch of the huge range of critical writing available.

TEXTUAL STUDY

When *The Prelude* was first published after Wordsworth's death, it received almost no attention from the critics. Ernest de Selincourt's scholarly labours on the text of the early version of this poem (1926) allowed a new kind of study of Wordsworth, focused around his autobiography. Textual critics started to disentangle the muddle of Wordsworth's changes to his poems, and construct an accurate chronology for their times of composition and publication. Formerly the dating of his poems had been obscured by Wordsworth's thematic arrangement of texts in his collected poems. The steady development of Wordsworth's thought and craft, sometimes mixed with a biographical approach, becomes the object of the critic's endeavour. R.D. Havens's *The Mind of Poet: A Study of Wordsworth's Thought with Particular Reference to* The Prelude (1941) is an example of this approach.

NEW CRITICISM AND AFTER

Matthew Arnold's desire to kick out the baggage of philosophical systems and bad poetry was a precursor of the so-called New Criticism of the

1930s and 1940s in the USA. New Critics sought to look at texts as autonomous items, divorced from literary, political and social history, or biographical background. In close readings of individual poems, these writers sought to reveal them as verbal structures bound together by ambiguity and irony: certain of Wordsworth's lyrics and sections of *The Prelude* are clearly well suited to this approach. No single major study devoted to Wordsworth emerged from this movement, though it generated innumerable essays on individual poems. This method of dealing with poems was perfect for the class-room and the lecture theatre, and, modified by a less absolute rigour with regard to the exclusion of interesting background material, it remains as a common foundation for the study of literature in schools, and indeed often informs the commentaries in student-aimed notes of this kind.

In Britain F.R. Leavis espoused the close textual study of literature of the New Critics, but was prepared to discuss literary history and influence, and added a moral and educational urgency to literary study which Arnold would have recognised. In *Revaluation* (1936) his essay on Wordsworth is wide-ranging, taking in a comparison of the language of the two versions of *The Prelude*, and examining the moral and psychological balance in the poet's work. Leavis, impressed by Wordsworth's seriousness, leaves his reputation intact, in contrast with the attack on Shelley in the same book, which led a generation of readers to ignore that poet.

BIOGRAPHICAL, PSYCHOLOGICAL AND HISTORICAL CRITICISM

Wordsworth's relationship with Annette Vallon was well know to his inner circle of friends – Henry Crabb Robinson, who was present when in 1820 Wordsworth introduced Mary Wordsworth to Annette Vallon, felt it 'indelicate' that Caroline called him 'father' – but these facts were lost till rediscovered by Emile Legouis and the American G.M. Harper who brought the matter to light in a series of articles and books from 1916 onwards. The disparity between Wordsworth's short intensely creative period, and his lengthy dullness perhaps could now be explained psychologically: was this caused by guilt? Herbert Read's *Wordsworth* (1930) argues this case.

Other psychological studies have followed; for example, F.W. Bateson's *Wordsworth: A Re-Interpretation* (1954) argues that the work is best understood in terms of the poet's half-repressed incestuous love for his sister Dorothy.

An off-shoot of progressively more detailed biographical data, and the changing historical understanding of the period in which Wordsworth lived, has allowed a number of different specialised approaches. F. M. Todd's *Politics and the Poet: A Study of Wordsworth* (1957) has since been superseded by work of the new historicist critics from the 1980s onwards, whose meticulously detailed examination of the political, social and literary milieu in which Wordsworth wrote has led to very detailed understanding of the relationship between his poetry, his beliefs, and history. *Wordsworth and Coleridge: The Radical Years* (1988) by Nicholas Roe is one such study. *Romantics, Rebels and Reactionaries: English Literature and its Background 1760–1830* (1982), by Marilyn Butler, is a magisterial and wide-ranging study of the period that places Wordsworth in relation to politics and literary and intellectual history.

CONTEMPORARY CRITICISM

The need in universities for university staff to produce research in the form of books and papers from the 1980s onwards has led to enormous quantities of critical writing being produced as part of the necessary career pattern of academics. Such material, most of it recondite in the extreme and of interest only to a few experts, has a short shelf life, being sold at full price for a few months and then remaindered. Wordsworth, as a 'site of contestation', is a mine for research of this kind. New methods of studying literature condemned Wordsworth out of hand for his lack of meaning in present-day society. Students were expected to have a grip on a number of twentieth-century intellectual movements – linguistics, psychoanalysis, the history of the study of literature in the academy, feminism, and so on – before they could understand a single poem by Wordsworth in its context, and such understanding would lead to the realisation that, for example, a lyric such as 'I wandered lonely as a cloud' is utterly irrelevant in a society that has rightly turned its back on a 'high' culture that was the property of the elite, and where popular culture was deemed the proper study for students, since it was everywhere available, of direct interest, and just as capable of bearing theorisation as poetry. It is possible to experience as much potential value in the discussion of *Star Trek* or *Big Brother* as in the literary relationships between an early nineteenth-century poet and his contemporaries.

Wordsworth, having concealed his affair and illegitimate daughter from the general public, and been tirelessly cared for by his sister and wife, was an obvious and easy target for early feminists. Dorothy's *Journal*, clearly, offered a more truthful illustration of sexual politics and the position of women than any poem by Wordsworth, and indeed exposed the poet as an idealist and exaggerator – the 'host of golden daffodils' is revealed in her account as merely a small clump. The silence of his other female companions may be seen as even more eloquent. Wordsworth's turning away from his early radicalism made him an apostate, not just for Byron and Shelley, but for Marxist and radical critics of the present day.

Aldous Huxley suggested in an essay, 'Wordsworth in the Tropics' (1926) that Wordsworth's attitude to Nature could not survive trans-plantation into different geographies and cultures. Writers and critics from English-speaking countries outside Britain came to see Wordsworth's essentialism as part of the cultural imperialism inherent in teaching poems about daffodils in Australia or Africa.

All these attacks were part of the proper dispute about what material should studied as 'English', a discussion in which the British government, in establishing a 'national curriculum', has felt it necessary to intervene. Many university departments have moved away entirely from teaching literature of the kind that Wordsworth represents. 'Cultural Studies' is now a common degree programme. Can anyone doubt that there are many more pressing things for young people to read and learn about than a small bundle of early nineteenth-century poems? Is Wordsworth anything other than an antiquarian interest, a single if weighty milestone in a discredited 'high culture'. Can the critics reinvent him again? Will Wordsworth survive in some form or other, as a writer still valued by readers in the twenty-first century?

In a critical movement called 'ecocriticism', a concern for the environment is the foundation of a new way of looking at literature. Jonathan Bate's *The Song of the Earth* (2001) is a key text in this new development, and places a special emphasis on poetry.

PART SIX

BROADER PERSPECTIVES

FURTHER READING

M.H. Abrams, *The Mirror and the Lamp*, 1953
Background to Romantic ideas

M.H. Abrams, *Natural Supernaturalism*, 1971
Background to Romantic ideas

James Averill, *Wordsworth and the Poetry of Human Suffering*, 1980

Juliet Barker, *Wordsworth, A Life*, 2000
Biography

Jonathan Bate, *The Song of the Earth*, 2001

F.W. Bateson, *Wordsworth: A Re-Interpretation*, 1954

John Beer, *Wordsworth and the Human Heart*, 1978

Marilyn Butler, *Romantics, Rebels and Reactionaries: English Literature and its Background 1760–1830*, 1982

Laurence Coupe, ed., *The Green Studies Reader: From Romanticism to Ecocriticism*, 2000

John Danby, *The Simple Wordsworth*, 1960

Stephen Gill, *William Wordsworth, A Life*, 1989
Biography

Stephen Gill, *Wordsworth and the Victorians*, 1998

Geoffrey Hartman, *Wordsworth's Poetry 1787–1814*, 1964

W.J. Harvey and Richard Gravil, eds., *The Prelude* (Casebook Series), 1972
Collected criticism

R.D. Havens, *The Mind of Poet: A Study of Wordsworth's Thought with Particular Reference to* The Prelude, 1941

K. R. Johnston, *The Hidden Wordsworth: Poet, Lover, Rebel, Spy*, 1998

John Jones, *The Egotistical Sublime*, 1954

A.R. Jones and W. Tydeman, eds., *Lyrical Ballads* (Casebook Series), 1972
Collected criticism

Celeste Langan, *Romantic Vagrancy: Wordsworth and the Simulation of Freedom*, 1995

F.R. Leavis, *Revaluation*, 1936
Now chiefly of interest as part of the history of critical debate

Herbert Lindenburger, *On Wordsworth's Prelude*, 1963

S.M. Parrish, *The Art of the Lyrical Ballads*, 1973

David Pirie, *The Poetry of Grandeur and Tenderness*, 1982

John Purkis, *A Preface to Wordsworth*, 2000

Herbert Read, *Wordsworth*, 1930

Robert Rehder, *Wordsworth and the Beginnings of Modern Poetry*, 1981

Nicholas Roe, *Wordsworth and Coleridge: The Radical Years*, 1988

Leslie Stephen, 'Wordsworth's Ethics', *Hours in a Library* (Third Series), 1879
Victorian statement of the consoling values of Wordsworth's philosophy

F. M. Todd, *Politics and the Poet: A Study of Wordsworth*, 1957

Leon Waldoff, *Wordsworth in His Major Lyrics: The Art and Psychology of Self-representation*, 2001

Robert Woof, *Wordsworth: The Critical Heritage*, 2001
Collected criticism

Dorothy Wordsworth, *The Grasmere and Alfoxden Journals*, ed. Pamela Woof, 2002

Jonathan Wordsworth, *William Wordsworth: The Borders of Vision*, 1982

Jonathan Wordsworth, ed., *The Prelude: The Four Texts*, 1995
Edition of the different versions of the poem

Duncan Wu, ed., *A Companion to Romanticism*, 1999

World events	Author's life	Literary events
1770 Cook discovers Australia	**1770** Wordsworth born at Cockermouth, Cumbria	**1770** Thomas Chatterton, poet, dies aged 18; Oliver Goldsmith *The Deserted Village*
		1774 Goethe, *The Sorrows of Young Werther*
1775 American War of Independence begins		
		1776 David Hume, philosopher, dies
1778 Britain declares war on France which has allied with American Colonists	**1778** Death of mother	
	1779 Attends Hawkshead Grammar School until 1787	
1781 William Pitt enters Parliament		**1781** Immanuel Kant, *Critique of Pure Reason*
		1782 Rousseau, *Confessions*
1783 American Colonies' independence recognised; Pitt's first ministry	**1783** Death of father	
1786 Mont Blanc climbed for first time		
	1787 Student at St John's College, Cambridge, until 1791	
1788 George III's first attack of madness		
1789 French Revolution begins; Declaration of the Rights of Man; fall of La Bastille		**1789** William Blake, *Songs of Innocence*
	1790 Walking tour of France, Switzerland and Italy	**1790** Edmund Burke, *Reflections on the Revolution in France*
	1791 Residence in London; Return to France	**1791** Thomas Paine, *The Rights of Man*

World events	Author's life	Literary events
1792 France becomes a Republic	**1792** Relationship with Annette Vallon; birth of daughter Caroline	**1792** Mary Wollstonecraft, *A Vindication of the Rights of Woman*
1793 France and Britain at war;execution of Louis XVI; Reign of Terror	**1793** Publishes *An Evening Walk* and *Descriptive Sketches*	**1793** William Godwin, *Inquiry Concerning Political Justice*
1794 Joseph Priestley emigrates to America (after rioters burn his laboratory); John Thelwall and other Jacobins tried for treason		**1794** Blake, *The Book of Urizen; Songs of Experience*
1795-9 France governed by Directoire	**1795** Left £900 by Calvert; meets Godwin and Coleridge	
	1796 Crisis of political beliefs and ideas	
	1798 Revisits Wye valley; With Coleridge, publishes *Lyrical Ballads;* Visits Germany with Coleridge; Starts writing his autobiographical poem, eventually to be published as *The Prelude*	
	1799 Settles in Lake District with sister Dorothy	**1799** Schiller, *Wallenstein*
1800 Napoleon defeats Austria in Battle of Marengo		**1800** William Cowper dies; Maria Edgeworth, *Castle Rackrent*
	1801 Second edition of *Lyrical Ballads* published	
1802 Peace of Amiens	**1802** Marries Mary Hutchinson	
1803 Britain renews war with France	**1803** Third edition of *Lyrical Ballads* published	
1804 Napoleon becomes Emperor; younger Pitt Prime Minister again		

World events	Author's life	Literary events
1805 Battle of Trafalgar	**1805** Brother John drowns	**1805** Walter Scott, *The Lay of the Last Minstrel*
1807 Slave trade abolished in British Empire	**1807** *Poems in Two Volumes* published	
1808 Peninsular War begins		**1808** Goethe, *Faust*
	1810 *Guide to the Lakes* published	**1810** Scott, *The Lady of the Lake*
		1811 Jane Austen, *Sense and Sensibility*
1812 Napoleon retreats from Moscow	**1812** Deaths of children Catherine and Thomas	**1812** Byron, *Childe Harold*
	1813 Appointed Distributor of Stamps for Westmorland	
	1814 *The Excursion*	**1814** Shelley, *Refutation of Deism*
1815 Battle of Waterloo	**1815** *Poems*; *The White Doe of Rylstone*	
		1817 Coleridge publishes *Biographia Literaria*
		1818 Mary Shelley, *Frankenstein*; Keats, *Endymion*
1819 Peterloo Massacre	**1819** *The Waggoner*; *Peter Bell*	**1819** Byron, *Don Juan*
1820 George III dies, George IV accedes	**1820** Visits the Continent; *Miscellaneous Poems* (four vols)	**1820** Keats, *Lamia, Isabella, Eve of St Agnes*
		1821 John Keats dies; Shelley, *Adonais*
	1822 *Ecclesiastical Sketches*	**1822** Shelley drowns; Thomas De Quincey, *Confessions of an English Opium Eater*
		1823 Carlyle, 'The Life of Schiller'; James Fenimore Cooper, *The Pioneers*
	1824 *Poetical Works* (four vols)	**1824** Lord Byron dies

World events	Author's life	Literary events
		1826 Cooper, *Last of the Mohicans*
	1829 Dorothy ill	
1830 George IV dies; William IV accedes; Louis-Philippe becomes 'citizen king' of France		
		1832 Tennyson, *Poems;* Scott and Goethe die
1834 Tolpuddle Martyrs transported to Australia; slavery abolished in British Empire		**1834** Harrison Ainsworth, *Rookwood;* Carlyle, *Sartor Resartus*
	1835 *Yarrow Revisited and Other Poems*	**1835** Coleridge dies
		1836 Ralph Waldo Emerson, *Nature*
1837 Accession of Queen Victoria (–1901)	**1837** Tours in France and Italy	**1837** Charles Dickens, *Pickwick Papers*
	1838 Awarded doctorate by Durham University	
	1839 Awarded doctorate by Oxford University	**1839** Stendhal: *The Charterhouse of Parma*
1840 Rowland Hill introduces penny post		
1842 Second Chartist petition rejected by the Commons	**1842** *Poems, Chiefly of Early and Late Years*; pension from Civil List of £300 p.a.	**1842** Browning: *Dramatic Lyrics* Tennyson: *Poems*
	1843 Appointed Poet Laureate	
1845 Famine in Ireland		**1845** Poe: *Tales of Mystery and Imagination*
1846 Peel repeals Corn Laws, allowing import of untaxed corn		**1847** Charlotte Brontë: *Jane Eyre* Emily Brontë: *Wuthering Heights*
1848 Revolutions in Europe; third Chartist petition fails		**1848** Thackeray: *Vanity Fair*
	1849 Final version of *Poetical Works* (six vols)	
	1850 Wordsworth dies; *The Prelude* published by wife and executors	

y

blank verse lines of unrhymed iambic pentameter, as used in Shakespeare's plays and Milton's *Paradise Lost*

dramatic monologue a poem built around a speech by a single speaker who is not the poet; there should be enough information for the reader to understand the kind of person who is speaking. This was one of the most influential forms for poetry in the nineteenth and twentieth centuries

emblem a symbolic or allegorical picture

epithets an adjective or adjectival phrase

first-person narrative narrative told from the point of view of an 'I'

foot a unit used in the discussion of metre, or the rhythm of verse. 'Feet' are combinations of stressed and unstressed syllables that cut across word-boundaries and grammar in an attempt to define the sound of the line when read out loud

genre a kind of literature, with its own characteristics, such as novel, tragedy, lyric, etc.

iambic an iambus is a metrical 'foot' consisting of an unstressed syllable followed by a stressed syllable: ti-tum

interlocutor the other person in a conversation or argument

inversion change to normal word-order, as for example, placing an adjective after the noun it qualifies

metaphor describing one thing as if it was another thing; a common feature of poetry

narrative a story; a connected series of events

pentameter a line of five 'feet' (iambic pentameter = ti-tum ti-tum ti-tum ti-tum ti-tum)

persona a mask or personality adopted by a poet or novelist, that may be a version of themselves, or a quite separate kind of person.

personification a special kind of metaphor in which a thing or an idea is turned into a person

poetic diction see Part Three, Critical Approaches

prospect poem a poem describing picturesque scenery; often used as a type of travel writing

quatrain a stanza of four lines

queer theory a critical approach examining literature from the point of view of homosexuals, after revealing the way in which homosexual interests and values have been either suppressed entirely, or expressed only in the margins of literary and critical texts

realism literature that presents itself as dealing with 'real' life, which is usually grim and unpleasant

rhetorical question a question that does not require or expect an answer; common in poetry

romantic a slippery word with a variety of meanings. At its weakest it simply means 'to do with love', or 'glamorous, because youthful and daring'. As a term from literary history it applies to poets writing between about 1790 and 1830 in England and Europe. The most famous writers commonly grouped under this term are Wordsworth, Coleridge, Keats, Shelley and Byron, though many critics argue that Wordsworth has little to do with the generation of 'Romantic' poets that followed him, and had his roots as a writer firmly in the eighteenth century. So-called 'Romantic' poets – who in many respects have little in common – are likely to exhibit in their work some or all of the following interests:

- The imagination, either as a way of apprehending things through the creative act of writing a poem, or as a mental world different from 'reality', even perhaps at odds with it
- Dreams and the artificial worlds created in writing
- Human feelings, very often perceived as in conflict with the powers of reason
- Nature
- The Self
- Rebellion against old ideas and systems of rules, whether social, political or literary

simile a kind of metaphor that works by the comparison of one thing to another, on the basis of a shared quality. The two things to be compared are always linked by the words 'as' or 'like'

sententious language which aims at a weighty and impressive sense of judgement

sentimental bestowing more feeling on a subject than it is worth

stanza a regular group of lines in a piece of verse

symbol something which stands for other ideas and things, as well as for itself; a common feature of poetry

tenor that which is described in a metaphor

tetrameter in verse, a line of four 'feet' (iambic tetrameter = ti-tum ti-tum ti-tum ti-tum)

tone the manner or mood adopted by a writer to subject matter

trimeter in verse, a line of three 'feet' (iambic trimeter = ti-tum ti-tum ti-tum)

vehicle that idea or object that is used to describe the 'tenor' of a metaphor

vignette a little picture of a thing or group of things

Martin Gray has worked as a lecturer in various universities in Britain and abroad. From 1994 to 1996 he was head of the Department of Literary Studies at the University of Stirling in Scotland. He is the author two companion volumes to the York Notes series, *A Dictionary of Literary Terms* (York Handbooks, Longman, 1984 and 1992) and *A Chronology of English Literature* (York Handbooks, Longman, 1989). He is General Editor of York Notes Advanced.

Notes

Notes

NOTES

Notes

NOTES

York Notes Advanced

Margaret Atwood
Cat's Eye

Margaret Atwood
The Handmaid's Tale

Jane Austen
Emma

Jane Austen
Mansfield Park

Jane Austen
Persuasion

Jane Austen
Pride and Prejudice

Jane Austen
Sense and Sensibility

Alan Bennett
Talking Heads

William Blake
*Songs of Innocence and of
Experience*

Charlotte Brontë
Jane Eyre

Charlotte Brontë
Villette

Emily Brontë
Wuthering Heights

Angela Carter
Nights at the Circus

Geoffrey Chaucer
*The Franklin's Prologue and
Tale*

Geoffrey Chaucer
The Miller's Prologue and Tale

Geoffrey Chaucer
*Prologue to the Canterbury
Tales*

Geoffrey Chaucer
*The Wife of Bath's Prologue
and Tale*

Samuel Taylor Coleridge
Selected Poems

Joseph Conrad
Heart of Darkness

Daniel Defoe
Moll Flanders

Charles Dickens
Bleak House

Charles Dickens
Great Expectations

Charles Dickens
Hard Times

Emily Dickinson
Selected Poems

John Donne
Selected Poems

Carol Ann Duffy
Selected Poems

George Eliot
Middlemarch

George Eliot
The Mill on the Floss

T.S. Eliot
Selected Poems

T.S. Eliot
The Waste Land

F. Scott Fitzgerald
The Great Gatsby

E.M. Forster
A Passage to India

Brian Friel
Translations

Thomas Hardy
Jude the Obscure

Thomas Hardy
The Mayor of Casterbridge

Thomas Hardy
The Return of the Native

Thomas Hardy
Selected Poems

Thomas Hardy
Tess of the d'Urbervilles

Seamus Heaney
*Selected Poems from Opened
Ground*

Nathaniel Hawthorne
The Scarlet Letter

Homer
The Iliad

Homer
The Odyssey

Aldous Huxley
Brave New World

Kazuo Ishiguro
The Remains of the Day

Ben Jonson
The Alchemist

James Joyce
Dubliners

John Keats
Selected Poems

Christopher Marlowe
Doctor Faustus

Christopher Marlowe
Edward II

Arthur Miller
Death of a Salesman

John Milton
Paradise Lost Books I & II

Toni Morrison
Beloved

George Orwell
Nineteen-Eighty-Four

Sylvia Plath
Selected Poems

Alexander Pope
*Rape of the Lock and other
poems*

William Shakespeare
Antony and Cleopatra

William Shakespeare
As You Like It

William Shakespeare
Hamlet

William Shakespeare
King Lear

William Shakespeare
Macbeth

William Shakespeare
Measure for Measure

William Shakespeare
The Merchant of Venice

William Shakespeare
*A Midsummer Night's
Dream*

William Shakespeare
Much Ado About Nothing

William Shakespeare
Othello

William Shakespeare
Richard II

William Shakespeare
Richard III

William Shakespeare
Romeo and Juliet

William Shakespeare
The Taming of the Shrew

William Shakespeare
The Tempest

William Shakespeare
Twelfth Night

William Shakespeare
The Winter's Tale

George Bernard Shaw
Saint Joan

Mary Shelley
Frankenstein

Jonathan Swift
Gulliver's Travels and A Modest Proposal

Alfred, Lord Tennyson
Selected Poems

Virgil
The Aeneid

Alice Walker
The Color Purple

Oscar Wilde
The Importance of Being Earnest

Tennessee Williams
A Streetcar Named Desire

Jeanette Winterson
Oranges Are Not the Only Fruit

John Webster
The Duchess of Malfi

Virginia Woolf
To the Lighthouse

W.B. Yeats
Selected Poems

Metaphysical Poets

GCSE and equivalent levels

Maya Angelou
I Know Why the Caged Bird Sings

Jane Austen
Pride and Prejudice

Alan Ayckbourn
Absent Friends

Elizabeth Barrett Browning
Selected Poems

Robert Bolt
A Man for All Seasons

Harold Brighouse
Hobson's Choice

Charlotte Brontë
Jane Eyre

Emily Brontë
Wuthering Heights

Shelagh Delaney
A Taste of Honey

Charles Dickens
David Copperfield

Charles Dickens
Great Expectations

Charles Dickens
Hard Times

Charles Dickens
Oliver Twist

Roddy Doyle
Paddy Clarke Ha Ha Ha

George Eliot
Silas Marner

George Eliot
The Mill on the Floss

Anne Frank
The Diary of Anne Frank

William Golding
Lord of the Flies

Oliver Goldsmith
She Stoops to Conquer

Willis Hall
The Long and the Short and the Tall

Thomas Hardy
Far from the Madding Crowd

Thomas Hardy
The Mayor of Casterbridge

Thomas Hardy
Tess of the d'Urbervilles

Thomas Hardy
The Withered Arm and other Wessex Tales

L.P. Hartley
The Go-Between

Seamus Heaney
Selected Poems

Susan Hill
I'm the King of the Castle

Barry Hines
A Kestrel for a Knave

Louise Lawrence
Children of the Dust

Harper Lee
To Kill a Mockingbird

Laurie Lee
Cider with Rosie

Arthur Miller
The Crucible

Arthur Miller
A View from the Bridge

Robert O'Brien
Z for Zachariah

Frank O'Connor
My Oedipus Complex and Other Stories

George Orwell
Animal Farm

J.B. Priestley
An Inspector Calls

J.B. Priestley
When We Are Married

Willy Russell
Educating Rita

Willy Russell
Our Day Out

J.D. Salinger
The Catcher in the Rye

William Shakespeare
Henry IV Part 1

William Shakespeare
Henry V

William Shakespeare
Julius Caesar

William Shakespeare
Macbeth

William Shakespeare
The Merchant of Venice

William Shakespeare
A Midsummer Night's Dream

William Shakespeare
Much Ado About Nothing

William Shakespeare
Romeo and Juliet

William Shakespeare
The Tempest

William Shakespeare
Twelfth Night

George Bernard Shaw
Pygmalion

Mary Shelley
Frankenstein

R.C. Sherriff
Journey's End

Rukshana Smith
Salt on the Snow

John Steinbeck
Of Mice and Men

Robert Louis Stevenson
Dr Jekyll and Mr Hyde

Jonathan Swift
Gulliver's Travels

Robert Swindells
Daz 4 Zoe

Mildred D. Taylor
Roll of Thunder, Hear My Cry

Mark Twain
Huckleberry Finn

James Watson
Talking in Whispers

Edith Wharton
Ethan Frome

William Wordsworth
Selected Poems

A Choice of Poets

Mystery Stories of the Nineteenth Century including The Signalman

Nineteenth Century Short Stories

Poetry of the First World War

Six Women Poets